MW01485045

"Digital transformation is an
Stijn Viaene skillfully guides
embrace the digital revolu
successful business leaders of tomorrow."
Johan Thijs, *CEO at KBC Group*

"If you're wondering how to lead your company into the digital age,
this book is a lucid and pragmatic best friend. How to unite strategy *and*
digital transformation, people *and* technology, exploiting *and* exploring
innovation, the established *and* the disruptive? It maps your route
to leading transformation. A treasure hunt!"
Stephanie Hottenhuis, *Chair of the Board of Management*
at KPMG in the Netherlands

"You cannot buy your way out of digital disruption. You need a willingness
to discover, an ambitious strategy, the courage to let go and the audacity
to connect in profoundly different ways. Stijn's book is a powerful summary
of the road we've travelled together, and which is far from over."
Peter Oosterveer, *CEO at Arcadis*

"This book is your guide to remodelling your business into one that is ready
to compete and thrive in the digital age. Using plain and simple language,
illustrated with selected case studies, the book provides a clear road map in
what to consider before taking on the transformation journey and the steps
to take after you embark on it. Highly recommended!"
Frans Muller, *President & CEO at Royal Ahold Delhaize NV*

"Stijn Viaene pieced together a great work on digital transformation.
He provides the essential inspiration for building a framework and common
language to collaboratively change our ways of working. The book gives you
the confidence and energy to contribute to a better future as opposed
to becoming a victim of technology."
Jean-Christophe Tellier, *CEO at UCB*

First edition: 2020

Published by
Uitgeverij Acco, Blijde Inkomststraat 22, 3000 Leuven, Belgium
Email: uitgeverij@acco.be – Website: www.acco.be

The Netherlands:
Acco Nederland, Westvlietweg 67 F, 2495 AA Den Haag, The Netherlands
Email: info@uitgeverijacco.nl – Website: www.accouitgeverij.nl

Cover design: XPair
Typesetting: Xpair

D/2020/0543/36   NUR 801   ISBN 978-94-6379-813-6

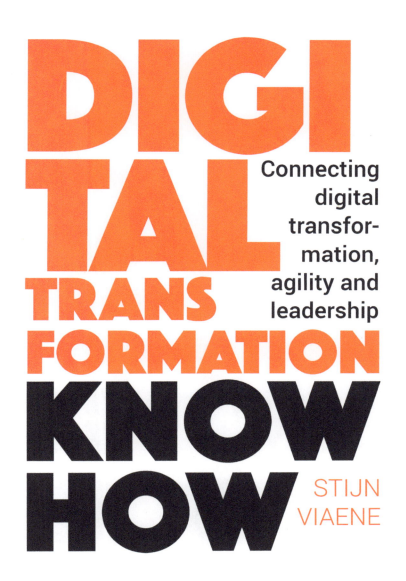

DIGITAL TRANS FORMATION KNOW HOW

Connecting digital transfor- mation, agility and leadership

STIJN VIAENE

acco

CONTENTS

POINT OF VIEW IS VIEW IS WORTH 80 IQ POINTS

Alan Kay

PREFACE

Over the period 2017 to 2019, I wrote several pieces on digital transformation for The European Business Review and Ivey Business Journal. I was on a mission to make "digital transformation", i.e. a form of end-to-end, integrated business transformation where digital technologies play a dominant role, understandable to a broad business audience.

In the first article, I synthesised my views on digital transformation from several years of working with digital transformation practitioners and their organisations. I wanted to describe the leadership challenges involved in digital transformation, and I did so by bringing the notion of "organisational agility" into the mix – i.e. an organisation's capacity to routinely explore and exploit opportunities faster than its rivals. The article was featured on The European Business Review's cover in May 2017.

After that first article, I wrote several more. Each addressed digital transformation in more depth. Each started from a particular question, such as "How to rethink strategy for the digital age?" and "How to make sense of customer experience as the new normal for value creation?" After the final article about scaling agility was published, I felt that it would be worthwhile to release the contents of the articles as a bundle, which eventually gave rise to this book about digital transformation.

The idea of writing a book about digital transformation had been in my mind for a while. But I had convinced myself that I was not "a book author" ... I was more of "an article man". After all, writing articles is how I earned my spurs as an academic. Until this bundle of articles made sense. During the Summer of 2019, I felt the closure I was looking for. Drawing on several years of research and in-depth case studies, I had found a way to create a book that would get the job done:

- Allow readers to speak about digital transformation with more understanding.
- Help them frame digital transformation as a leadership challenge to create organisational agility.
- Give them the confidence to get involved in digital transformation as actors, rather than as bystanders or victims.

What started out as a bundle of articles became so much more. I have significantly upgraded the original article content. I added even more examples and mini-cases, including experiences from banking, media, energy, bio-pharmaceuticals, construction, government and more. Most importantly, by rearranging the articles, I created a storyline that culminates in linking digital transformation, organisational agility and leadership, in a practical way. I added an introduction to address the "Digital transformation, so what?" question, before tackling the "Now what?" in the chapters that follow. Having a good grasp of the context that gives rise to the need for digital transformation helps to align the troops and overcome important barriers to change.

In 2014, Vlerick Business School (Belgium), where I have been a professor for more than 16 years, was one of the first European business schools to launch an open executive programme on digital transformation. We called it the Digital Leadership Summer School, an immersive five-day experience featuring lectures, cases, guests, games and discussions. When my colleagues and I conceived the Summer School, there were some competing programmes at other business schools, but very few dealt with transformation. Instead, most of them largely ignored the existing enterprise and concentrated on creating something completely new. However, for the organisations I was working with, taking this path usually seemed neither very practical nor very wise.

The position I took then and now still, is that organisations that haven't grown up digitally aren't automatically lost. In other words, rather than starting from scratch, there is a path to success that takes the existing enterprise as the starting point. Evolving your current business to win in the digital age puts you in the scenario of digital transformation – and that's where most of my work on digital transformation has been ever since.

Alan Kay, American computer scientist and winner of the 2003 A.M. Turing Award, once noted: "Point of view is worth 80 IQ points."[1] I couldn't agree more. A lack of perspective and a common language are primary reasons why so many people and organisations continue to struggle with digital transformation. This book offers a frame of reference to anyone who is looking for a grounded, practical perspective on making digital transformations work.

I wish you an interesting read.

Stijn Viaene

THE REAL PUZZLE
INVOLVED IN DIGITAL
TRANSFORMATION
IS DISCOVERING
A FUNDAMENTALLY
NEW RELATIONSHIP
BETWEEN PEOPLE
AND TECHNOLOGY

DIGITAL TRANSFORMATION, SO WHAT?

In their book, *The Second Machine Age*,[1] Erik Brynjolfsson and Andrew McAfee, argue that we are at an inflexion point in time, entering the second machine age. Digital technologies, i.e. those that work to turn information into the ones and zeroes that are the native language of computers and their kin, are transforming society and the economy. This new era is not just different. It is better, due to increased variety and volume of consumption, more choice and freedom, where abundance is the norm. Digital technologies have caused a paradigm shift.

The Industrial Revolution, a series of major developments in science, technology and mechanical engineering in the late 18th and early 19th centuries, was spurred by the invention and subsequent improvement of James Watt's steam engine and ushered in the first machine age. Just as the steam engine enabled us to overcome the limitations of human and animal muscle power, in the second machine age, digital technology will help us to transcend the limitations of human brainpower.

It took several generations to perfect the steam engine to power the Industrial Revolution. It has taken time, though significantly less, to perfect digital technologies. For example, over the past years, 3D digital printing has taken off, ready to revolutionise the manufacturing process in a variety of industries, from healthcare to construction and transportation. In 2011, IBM's computer system

Watson illustrated that artificial intelligence (AI) can beat humans at their game.[2] Today, AI – encompassing a set of disciplines including optimisation, speech and image recognition, natural language understanding, and more – provides machines with the capacity to imitate intelligent human behaviour. Humanoid robots and self-driving cars are now a reality.

Where we find ourselves, at this inflexion point, of a changing age may be too difficult for many people to comprehend. "When people look at the implications of ongoing exponential growth, it gets harder and harder [for them] to accept. So, you get people who really accept, yes, things are progressing exponentially, but they fall off the horse at some point because the implications are too fantastic",[3] according to famous futurist and inventor Ray Kurzweil. Kurzweil's bestseller, *The Singularity is Near*,[4] prompted Microsoft's Bill Gates in 2005 to call him "the best person I know at predicting the future of AI".[5]

This singularity refers to a hypothetical moment where technological progress is so rapid that it completely outstrips humans' ability to comprehend it. It represents a future during which technological advance will be so fast, and its impact so deep, that human life will be irreversibly transformed and beyond which events may become unpredictable. That future is nearer than we think, says Kurzweil:[6]

> *"By the time we get to the 2040s, we'll be able to multiply human intelligence a billionfold. That will be a profound change that's singular in nature. Computers are going to keep getting smaller and smaller. Ultimately, they will go inside our bodies and brains and make us healthier, make us smarter."*

Kurzweil's advocacy of an optimistic and transhumanist future continues to inspire innovators around the globe. Some are more cautious and point out the risks that we are facing. Pessimists like to paint a Terminatoresque picture of the apocalyptic moment when machines take over from humans. Generally, both optimists and pessimists make valid points. In essence, it is up to us to create a positive and voluntarist synthesis in a time of unprecedented opportunity and turbulence.

More digital turbulence ahead

It is widely acknowledged that the most critical challenge for companies today is dealing with their turbulent environments. This turbulence refers to the rapid and unpredictable changes in the business environment that affect a company's ability to create value. Two factors affect turbulence: complexity (i.e. the number, strength and dissimilarity of external forces or pressures) and volatility (i.e. the predictability and rate of change of the external forces or pressures). The more turbulent the environment, the more difficult it becomes for decision-makers to make winning choices.

Turbulence is common to all eras. Think of, for example, how wars, depressions, or oil shocks have affected the lives of firms. Think of industrialisation and globalisation forces, or climate change.

Over the last decades, however, we've experienced entirely new forms of turbulence, catalysed by emergent digital technologies. Think, for example, of the innovation[7] coming out of Silicon Valley, or of today's exciting fintech[8] competition. Think of effects on our economic and social systems of companies like Google, Facebook, Alibaba or Tencent. Think of privacy concerns, of fake news, of the war for talent, job creation and job loss in digital times. The effects of readily available digital technologies on complexity and volatility in social and business environments are very tangible.

Not all of this digital turbulence is bad. Some of its effects are amazing. Digital turbulence creates the context for inspirational developments, like decoding the human genome, self-driving cars, drones, augmented reality, etc. And yet, what we are experiencing today in terms of opportunities and threats is just the beginning. We shall see many more examples of digital turbulence over the coming decades; some good, some bad, and hopefully not too many ugly ones.

As this digital turbulence is the new normal, "old organisations" will need to get to grips with it. Or die. But how? Should they be afraid? Or should they be looking to the future with excitement?

Big bang disruptors don't waste time

Disruption, i.e. new entrants overthrowing the power structure in established industries by introducing far superior business models,[9] has been a recurring phenomenon since the dawn of the industrial age. Innovation and strategy expert Clayton Christensen from the Harvard Business School has devoted most of his career to answering the question why incumbents, established and respected companies, frequently miss out on new waves of innovation and are toppled by disruptors with superior designs for creating and capturing value.[10] Why is that? Do these former winners, innovators of the past, not see it coming?

Researchers have put forward several hypotheses; some referring to stupidity, complacency or management arrogance, others to barriers to responding efficiently such as legacy culture, organisation or technology. Christensen, however, suggested competence, rather than incompetence, as a root cause of incumbents getting toppled. These companies do have access to the best and brightest professionals, to the newest technologies. They have ample resources. It is the nature of their resource allocation, however, not scarcity that holds them back. Incumbents are not focused on creating radically new growth. Their best customers are happy, their short-term profitability targets guaranteed. The safer option of continuing down the travelled path, getting even better at what they already do best, is more appealing to investors and management. Scenario's for deeper, future-proof change and self-disruption are put in the fridge. They don't see a burning platform. They think they have time.

Time, however, is a precious commodity in the digital age. That is the point Larry Downes and Paul Nunes make when describing the emergence of "big bang disruptors".[11] They refer to digital ventures like Coursera and Khan Academy in education, WeChat and WhatsApp in mobile communication, Uber and Didi Chuxing in transportation. These entrepreneurial ventures come with radically new solutions to customer problems by fully embracing the innovative power of digital technologies. They could pop up from nowhere and wipe out entire established businesses in no time, the authors argue. Disruption could come from anywhere, from far beyond the borders of what you consider to be your industry or business model.

In Downes and Nunes' big bang world, incumbents no longer have the time, nor the capabilities, to rethink themselves. Established recipes for disciplined strategising, careful product marketing and innovation are utterly useless. An overstatement not entirely supported with the evidence produced by the authors, but Downes and Nunes' big bang disruption hypothesis and vivid examples have the merit of making their readers acutely aware of the broader management challenge of dealing with digital turbulence. Digital disruption is coming your way too, and it's probably going to be there faster than you expect.

Digital innovation is combinatorial

Big bang disruptors truly understand the pattern of innovation in the digital world. This pattern is rooted in the ubiquity of computing power and connectivity, and in information being able to flow freely. For sure, these ubiquities and free flows are not absolutes, but close enough to be workable hypotheses for digital innovation in many contexts.

The pattern of digital innovation roughly goes as follows:

- Over time, sensors and computers become exponentially cheaper, and smaller, making it affordable to include them everywhere. Thanks to this ubiquity in computing, every knowledge domain gets expressed in the language native to computers.
- Ubiquitous connectivity democratises access to knowledge domains; information is shared and reused at will.
- Entrepreneur-developers combine information freely, generating innovative business models that are both cheaper and better than anything that exists. Smart combination, rather than invention, fuels innovation.
- Industry boundaries do not matter. The status quo in existing industries is disrupted.

For example, digital disrupters Airbnb and Uber were born out of this pattern. They constitute powerful illustrations of significant new-value creation opportunities in a world where it has become economical to decouple information about physical resources from their physical carriers. Neither Airbnb nor Uber have a track record as brilliant technology inventors. Instead, they are masters at *combining* a diversity of readily available technology and information resources from a variety of sources to create new digital business models. Playing this combinatorial innovation game allows them to disrupt existing industries.[12]

Worldwide, the role of digital innovation hubs like Silicon Valley – i.e. vibrant and diverse actor communities or ecosystems that foster technological trends, collaborative innovation, and domain-specific insights – cannot be overstated in regard to the coming of age of this pattern of combinatorial digital innovation. The culture of generating winning combinations is what makes Silicon Valley so successful, according to leadership expert Rosabeth Moss Kanter of the Harvard Business School:[13]

> *"[The term] 'ecosystem' conveys the idea that all the pieces of an economy [including technology companies, financiers, talent, universities, government and more] come together in particular places, and that their strength and interactions determine prosperity and economic growth. In Silicon Valley there is a sense that you prosper only because you're surrounded by lots of resources that make it possible to succeed, beyond what your own entity controls. Think of it as your garden, where you need fertile soil, seeds, and other ingredients to make things grow."*

Considering digital transformation

Here's a timely question: If you are not a digital startup, a potential big bang disruptor, are you automatically lost?

You are not. Established companies are not lost by default. Evolving your current business to win in the digital age puts you in the scenario of digital transformation.

Big bang disruptors are inspirational as well as confrontational. They are crucial competitive benchmarks at the edge of the possible. Still, there is an alternative route to reinvent existing organisations that does not require you to throw the baby out with the bathwater.

It's the path that takes the existing enterprise as the starting point; strengthening existing capabilities and leveraging (possibly dormant) digital resources, rather than starting from scratch.

To succeed, however, you will have to accept that your established enterprise was not built to compete in a world that requires blending the physical and the digital seamlessly. You'll need to open yourself to the digital space to rediscover the nature of value creation, the critical capabilities that need to be grown, and the new skills that need to be developed. You'll have to integrate and internalise the new essential external complexity into your organisation as new patterns of working, and get rid of all the accidental complexity of the past; that was once essential but is now holding you back.

Finding new patterns of working which help you adapt to the digital environment and internalise its dynamics will be a learning process. There is no standard cookbook. What works for one organisation may not work for you, and vice versa. Starting from scratch implies a different trajectory than aiming to leverage your current enterprise. Transformation is path-dependent. You'll have to figure out the new patterns for yourself from learning by doing.

Don't be fooled by the label: Digital transformations are first and foremost business transformations. Where in the past information technology (IT) and process re-engineering programmes were often framed as cost, efficiency or productivity efforts, successful digital transformations are framed as business investments that target future-proof growth.

A digital transformation is a form of end-to-end, integrated business transformation where digital technologies play a dominant role. It is wise to discuss this definition up front. Make sure that all the stakeholders are on the same page about the nature of the change and the required decision making. Aside from reaching agreement on framing the business transformation for growth, also agree on its enterprise-wide nature. The forces of digital disruption will challenge the very fabric of your organisation. They will require synchronised interventions across the silos and impact all organisational design dimensions. Successful digital transformations are enterprise-wide by design.

Also agree on the dominant role of technology in digital transformation. You'll need to be on the offence, rather than the defence with your technology choices if you want to keep up with big bang disruptors. Stop saying that "technology is not the issue". This statement is in vogue and mostly accompanied by "people are". It emphasises the enormous reskilling, talent and cultural challenges ahead. Unfortunately, the slogan also misrepresents the real puzzle involved in digital transformation, that is discovering a fundamentally new relationship between people *and* technology. If you want to be a digital leader, you will need digital literacy as well as the ability to grow this transformative vision.

Four realities of digital competition

Before you start planning your digital transformation, you should make one simple commitment: Build digital into every initiative. Basically, every opportunity to capture the creative power of digital technologies should stand up to the following four realities of competing in a digital world:[14]

Reality 1: Customer experience is value

Products and services are no longer enough for gaining and retaining customers. Customer experience is vital. Customers need control over a seamless link of the physical and digital worlds. Empathy, deep contextual appreciation, and co-creation are essential factors in achieving that link.

Reality 2: Customers are moving targets

Customer attention is short-lived. As a result, brand loyalty is fragile. New mobile and social experiences are introduced at fleeting Internet speed. Customers switching between competing value propositions is the rule, rather than the exception. Data and analytics allow companies to successfully staple themselves to their customers' digital selves to stay relevant and appealing.

Reality 3: Business ecosystems co-create value

No one company possesses all the data, digital skills and capabilities to win over today's demanding and dynamic customers. Thinking in ecosystems is a powerful way to strategise about new combinatorial ways to create and capture value. It creates a fertile ground for digital partnerships, where different ecosystem actors bring their respective digital strengths together to grow the economic pie, not just split it.

Reality 4: Digital platforms boost value co-creation

Your digital innovation strength is limited by your ability to combine your digital resources with those of others. Today's most valuable and successful business ecosystems are enabled by digital platforms that boost combinatorial digital innovation. These carefully managed architectures of reusable digital resources empower you to capture opportunities faster than your competitors.

All four of these realities are addressed by big bang disruptors when they deploy digital technologies. For a solid competitive edge in the digital world, you need to do the same.

Use the four realities as your yardstick the next time you appraise an innovative idea, assess a project proposal, review a portfolio or roadmap. Challenge your teams to achieve all four. Consistent and systematic digital transformation is the key to compete significantly in the digital world. To succeed, you need to learn and build digital capabilities progressively, project by project.

What's next

With the context specified, it's time to get to work on *your* digital transformation. The following chapters provide a practical perspective on critical elements of successful digital transformation design: strategy for the digital age, customer experience design, data and analytics, digital partnership strategies, digital transformation leadership, and scaling agility. The book is built up in the following way:

Chapter 1 – Rethinking strategy for the digital age

What is the essence of creating a vigilant strategic routine for digital transformation? And how do you go about defining your digital operating model?

Chapter 2 – Digital reality no.1: Customer experience is value

Customer experience is a non-trivial value concept. Design thinking offers a useful framework for creating this value and is especially popular with digital entrepreneurs. What is it, and what does it entail?

Chapter 3 – How to catch a moving target

Data and analytics capabilities enable you to offer a continuation of valuable customer experiences, which is essential to deal with the moving targets your customers are. How do you go about building these analytics capabilities?

Chapter 4 – Digital partnership strategies revealed

If combinatorial digital innovation is the new standard, partnering is a logical thing to do. Which mindset and lens should you adopt? And how do you make partnering worth your while?

Chapter 5 – What digital leadership does

Leading digital transformation is a matter of action, rather than position. It is about creating the requisite organisational agility to thrive digitally. What combination of leadership types do you need to make this possible?

Chapter 6 – Creating agility at scale

Agility needs to find its way into the entire organisation. What are the challenges in scaling organisational agility? What are the dos and don'ts?

DIGITAL TRANSFORMATION INVESTS IN STRENGTHENING THE CORE AND GROWING THE MORE

1

RETHINKING STRATEGY FOR THE DIGITAL AGE

Every year introduces new flavours of digital technology.[1] There is a constant temptation to jump onto the bandwagon out of hope or out of fear of being left behind. Hope and fear are strong drivers but make for bad advisors. If your digital transformation only focuses on the exciting, new digital technologies, and not on winning business logic, you will quickly find you have spent yourself to death. Launching a bunch of digital initiatives that go in all sorts of directions does not constitute transformation.

If you want to be successful, you need to rethink your business strategy for the new digital realities. Strategy, not technology *per se*, drives digital transformations. Without high intention at the outset, even the most sincere efforts won't make your transformation work. The ability to make bold though wise strategic choices of many alternatives, against the backdrop of a turbulent digital business environment, separates the winners from the losers.

Building your case for radical action

Recognising the set of new realities driving competition is the starting point for digital transformation, i.e.

- Customer experience is value.
- Customers are moving targets.
- Business ecosystems co-create value.
- Digital platforms boost value co-creation.

Take your time to understand the nature of value creation in the digital space, the capabilities that need to be built, both technological and business, and the skills that need to be developed because of those new realities. As management thinker Peter Drucker once emphasised:[2] "A time of turbulence is a dangerous time, but its greatest danger is a temptation to deny reality."

Navel-gazing organisations may miss new opportunities, be oblivious to competitors and misunderstand the needs of customers. What is needed instead is an exploratory outward-facing focus, with open-minded scouts and champions.

Force yourself to go out on discovery missions, let others inspire you with their scouting assignments, listen to the markets, experience the new normal. Invite external challengers, consultants, entrepreneurs and experts to act as drivers and disrupt traditional thinking. Celebrate when you find confrontational data that challenge constraints and the status quo.

Don't just accept what others oracle or preach. Those that succeed do their own critical environment analysis, get involved, are scouts, and then make their own research synthesis, addressing the following questions to build their case for radical action:

- What are the costs of doing nothing?
- Why are incremental improvements not enough?
- What benefits can we capture with radical transformation?

Successful organisations use this case for action to push for high ambitions, clear goals and ramp up the heat for business transformation.

Responding to multiple possible futures

It is one thing to understand that the world around your organisation is changing. It is an entirely different thing to cope with it effectively.

While there are many frameworks for business strategy, essentially the idea is always the same: Envision an ambitious, winning point of view on the future of the organisation, and then pull it back to the present and make choices about where and how to play to win. Also, define where not to play, and what not to do or stop doing. The next steps involve identifying core organisational capabilities[3] and determining what management systems are needed. The book *Playing to Win: How Strategy Really Works* by Alan Lafley, former chief executive officer of Procter & Gamble, and strategic advisor Roger Martin, for example, holds an insightful, practical guide to such a strategic approach.[4]

Formulating a business strategy essentially revolves around what you think will be winning resource allocation choices. However, in turbulent times, the future business environment is hard to predict. Once you have accepted this, you don't want to commit yourself to just one future, but look at multiple possible future scenarios for the business environment and be ready to win when one or the other materialises. Sustained competitive advantage will no longer be about positioning yourself for one future, but about making and keeping yourself ready to act in multiple possible ones.

Working with future scenarios, i.e. alternative world views, is a powerful way of allowing organisations to steer a course between the false confidence of a single strategy and the ambiguous hesitation of turbulent times. Scenario analysis is a useful strategic tool that helps you dream up possible alternative futures. Scenarios are typically generated as combinations of extreme outcomes for two or more most important but also most uncertain external forces.[5] For example, four scenarios can be generated from combining "government intervention" as high vs. low and "consumer collectivism" as high vs. low.

By developing alternative views of the future, you will evolve broader perspectives, challenge conventional strategic choices and realise that you may be completely wrong. As a digital leader, you will learn to accept that you don't have a crystal ball and that the future is uncertain. That is why you shouldn't commit to a possible future too easily.

Instead, you will design possible courses of strategic action, i.e. possible options to create and capture value (i.e. business models), for each of the identified future scenarios. Some of them you will choose to activate, some will be put in the waiting room, others will be dismissed. You will also build into your business strategy routine a constant awareness of next the strategic options, even if you have only just launched your latest strategy. This, of course, requires that you become vigilant for signals, even weak ones, revealing themselves to help you steer in one direction or another.

In sum: In turbulent times, business strategy will be less about positioning, and more about adaptively responding to signals which will be picked up along the way. Course correction needs to become routine, built into the strategy process rather than done only once or on an ad hoc basis.

MINI-CASE
KBC tackles disruption with strategic vigilance

In 2014, KBC, one of Europe's leading banks, chose for a strategy that addressed the disruptive impact of digital technologies.[6] The company decided to spend 250 million euros over the period 2014-2020 in Customer 2020, a digital transformation programme for its Belgian home market.[7]

Before making this commitment, intending to formulate a comprehensive strategic answer, KBC spent several months scrutinising its environment. It invited trend-watchers, technology gurus, consultants and academics to challenge the executive team's ideas about digital disruption.

Serious about making a compelling case for radical action, the executive team mandated a team of some 75 members from a variety of departments to assess KBC's digital readiness compared to emerging trends and best-in-class practices beyond the boundaries of the banking industry. The scouting team put together four fact books (i.e. on customer behaviour, competitor, technology and organising trends) that helped build a credible and robust case for transformation.

From the analysis, the executives concluded that KBC had to defend its leading position, as well as embrace new opportunities for the future. The scouting team put forward five alternative world views. These scenarios corresponded with possible business model response options (see Figure 1).[8]

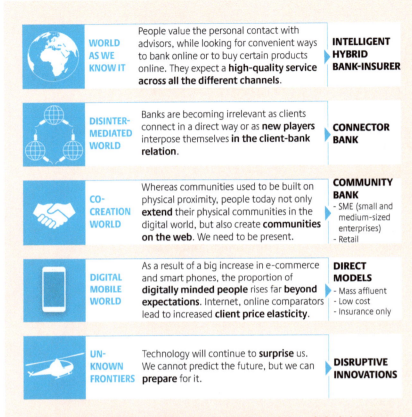

	WORLD AS WE KNOW IT	People value the personal contact with advisors, while looking for convenient ways to bank online or to buy certain products online. They expect a **high-quality service across all the different channels**.	**INTELLIGENT HYBRID BANK-INSURER**
	DISINTER-MEDIATED WORLD	Banks are becoming irrelevant as clients connect in a direct way or as **new players** interpose themselves **in the client-bank relation**.	**CONNECTOR BANK**
	CO-CREATION WORLD	Whereas communities used to be built on physical proximity, people today not only **extend** their physical communities in the digital world, but also create **communities on the web**. We need to be present.	**COMMUNITY BANK** - SME (small and medium-sized enterprises) - Retail
	DIGITAL MOBILE WORLD	As a result of a big increase in e-commerce and smart phones, the proportion of **digitally minded people** rises far **beyond expectations**. Internet, online comparators lead to increased **client price elasticity**.	**DIRECT MODELS** - Mass affluent - Low cost - Insurance only
	UN-KNOWN FRONTIERS	Technology will continue to **surprise** us. We cannot predict the future, but we can **prepare** for it.	**DISRUPTIVE INNOVATIONS**

Figure 1. Alternative banking business scenarios and their business model response options[9]

KBC decided to focus its digital efforts on strengthening its existing branch-based model to an omnichannel proposition; giving customers full control over their choice of channels with a promise of convenient, consistent access and tailored solutions (i.e. the "intelligent hybrid bank-insurer" business model option). At the same time, however, the bank decided to launch a selection of strategic experiments addressing alternative future scenarios. For example, KBC would offer convenient digital payment alternatives for local merchants and their customers to keep them close and to avoid being disintermediated (i.e. the "connector bank" business model option). It would also set up digital communities for starters and farmers and provide each of these groups with advice and money (i.e. the "community bank" business model option). A "direct" business model would be created for its Walloon sister company CBC.

Every six-month project wave of the Customer 2020 programme was informed by an environmental scanning for threats and opportunities, allowing the executive team to revisit investment options regularly. Johan Thijs, KBC Group's chief executive officer:[10]

> *"The options are put on the table regularly and re-evaluated within the parameters of where the environment is moving. Each time, we ask ourselves if this or that is a bet we want to take now. We try to anticipate, with a horizon of one to two years, by gathering data, carefully monitoring what is going on around us, and distilling trends. We then decide to try things. Some of it works, some doesn't. We accept this. What's important is that we keep a finger on the pulse and can regularly evaluate."*

The threat of digital disruption made KBC adopt a routine for seeking strategic advantage that was fundamentally mindful of the environmental turbulence. The executive team allowed themselves to activate options for multiple future scenarios. As they travelled down each of the paths, they started learning, tried to respond flexibly to what they learned, looking for ways to influence the underlying success variables.

Strategy as a portfolio of real options

Rethinking your business strategy to thrive in a turbulent digital economy will materialise as an investment portfolio of real options. These options will represent various business model choices, all aimed at growing your business by taking advantage of the creative power of digital technologies.

Why *real* options? Because in turbulent environments like the digital economy, strategic decisions can no longer be based on static business cases followed mindlessly, but rather involve learning by doing, active decision making. In this paradigm, strategy frames future decisions through compelling, robust business visioning and creating business purpose, but at the same time builds in the opportunity for intervening based on actual feedback.

Some of the options for creating and capturing value that you will make real in your growth portfolio will be closer to your current core business; others will be further off. In fact, you can look at your portfolio as composed of three broad option categories, with the risk-reward profile of each quite different:

- Strengthen the core, i.e. defend and grow the current core business.
- Extend the core, i.e. create adjacent growth.
- Self-disrupt, i.e. create radically new growth.[11]

Self-disruption requires you to go entirely outside the box. That is, your current business model(s) will no longer act as the context for strategising about how to create and capture value. You will allow yourself to think and act like a new digital entrant who has the ambition to radically innovate the business model(s). Alternatives one and two, i.e. strengthening and extending the core, by contrast, entertain options that start with the intention of building upon your current competitive strengths and business model(s).

Strengthening the core demands more of a business improvement or re-engineering mindset and skills. You'll embrace digital technologies for fruitful integration within your current core business model(s). Actually, you have a double aim: Lose the fat while growing the muscle. You want to keep only those elements that really add value so that you can fully focus on achieving profitable core growth.

For example: Dutch telecommunications company (telco) KPN initiated a digital transformation in 2014, after a financially and operationally hectic year.[12] It formulated a bold ambition to become the best service provider in the Netherlands, with an "un-telco-like high" net promoter score (NPS).[13] The pillars of the transformation strategy for the first two to three years were: (1) to strengthen customer relationships, network and IT; (2) to simplify products, processes andsystems; and (3) to grow customer loyalty. That is, KPN decided to focus on strengthening its core business first.

By the end of 2015, KPN had cut the number of product propositions by 75% in business-to-consumer (B2C) and by 35% in business-to-business (B2B). Run-rate savings had accumulated to some 280 million euros. Interestingly, KPN had also instituted a three-year freeze on new product launches, giving itself time to radically simplify its products, back-end processes and systems. Bouke Hoving, chief information officer at KPN:[14]

"Portfolio simplification risked dramatically affecting product lines and revenues. However, we spent a lot of time sharing details with the business units about the programme and the commercial possibilities. For example, simplifying the portfolio could help us to gain market share because it facilitated sales. Simplifying processes would allow us to cut [key product] order handling from half an hour to minutes in our retail stores. In fact, we saw the NPS very quickly go up and we reversed the negative trend for retail market shares."

To simplify and standardise back-end processes, KPN used a comprehensive industry-agreed processes architecture framework (i.e. TM Forum's eTOM[15] standard). The idea of using this back-end standard was two-fold: To combine the framework with its own new, digital-first front-end customer (experience) journeys, and to remake its back-end into an architecture of conveniently reusable digital resource components. Application programming interfaces (APIs) – combinations of software protocols, routines and tools – were used to provide access to digital resources, making it easier for developers to use them as a building block in new software applications.

Extending the core calls for a resource leveraging (i.e. *sharing*) mindset and skills. That is, you aim to reuse existing digital resources as building blocks for new growth options in areas related to, but not part of the current core.

> For example, when global biopharmaceutical company UCB introduced its new Patient Value Strategy in 2015, it stimulated innovation teams to experiment with taking internal data resources out of the context in which they originated, and combine them with external data resources for creating patient value adjacent to the current core business; that is "beyond the pill".[16]

As a rule, you can assume that there will be no extending the core without getting your core in order first. But mindfully investing in strengthening your current core can create major extension opportunities.

> For example, that was illustrated by KPN during 2017. That year, the telco established a partnership with Tencent, China's software giant, to launch the WeChat Go SIM card for Chinese tourists travelling in Europe. Bouke Hoving, chief information officer at KPN:[17]

"We had to compete [for winning the partnership with Tencent] against big European telcos, which offered further network capabilities. But we had superior software and IT capabilities. We were the only ones that could meet Tencent's challenging time-to-market requirements. We basically plugged our APIs directly into their system and were able to launch Europe-wide in weeks, not months. Also, it gave us a unique opportunity to co-develop the customer experience with Tencent. The partnership [was] extended to tourists travelling in Australia."

The collaboration with Tencent was an important digital transformation lighthouse project for KPN. That is, it was a highly visible, appealing, short-term project with well-defined and measurable outcomes, that served as a model of success for follow-up projects in the next stage of the transformation. Most notably, its success provided proof of the potential for using its newly architected back-end for generating new growth through combinatorial digital innovation with ecosystem partners, including those players that many had regarded as digital competitors.

Should you put digital evolution before digital revolution in allocating your resources? It is often worthwhile to start by thinking of evolution to prepare for big results with more revolutionary options. Looking at a portfolio of strategic options brings benefits. For example, an enterprise can try to build on the competitive strengths it has built up over the years, seeking profits and growth from its current core, while buying itself time for self-disruptive options to establish themselves. Just as wise investors diversify their financial portfolios, so will companies combine different digital growth options. The fundamental strategic choice then becomes what proportion of resources to allocate to each of the portfolio's categories.

Several factors, such as industry, competitive position and stage of development, have an impact on your company's ideal portfolio balance. Being wise, your choice will be determined by what your enterprise is and, especially, what you want it to be. What is your winning aspiration? What is your view on growth? What is your appetite for risk? Your answers to those questions decide your ideal portfolio balance.

Screening for real, win and worth

Not every growth option will turn out to be worthwhile pursuing. George Day's "real, win, worth it" (R-W-W) screen offers a simple set of questions to help you judge an option's strategic value:[18]

- Is there a real market for this opportunity?
  I.e. Is the market real? Is the product real?
- Can we gain and maintain a winning position?
  I.e. Can the product be competitive? Can our company be competitive?
- Will the expected return be worth the risks involved?
  I.e. Will the product be profitable at an acceptable risk level? Does launching the product make strategic sense?

Addressing these questions makes a big difference. In a world where access to technology is increasingly democratised, being first to launch a new technology has become less important than being the first to tap into new strategic growth areas.

MINI-CASE
Deseret News' dual transformation

The Internet changed everything for Deseret News, a
150-year-old newspaper published in Salt Lake City (UT). By
2008, Internet newcomers, such as Craigslist, Google and free
news websites were eroding every part of its revenue base.
From 2008 to 2010, Deseret News lost almost 30% of its print
display advertising and 70% of print classified revenues. Still,
at a time when several big-city newspapers were closed, Deseret
News managed to dodge the bullet.[19]

Deseret travelled a dual track, which chief executive officer
Clark Gilbert referred to as "Transformations A and B".
Transformation A aimed at strengthening the newspaper's
core. That meant focusing on only those aspects that
guaranteed profitable growth: A local daily paper providing
in-depth coverage of issues related to family and faith. At the
same time, a weekly print publication was added with the same
focus but aimed at a national audience. The weekly publication
could sell higher-margin national ads to compensate for the
revenue loss from local advertisers. Overall costs of the print
business were cut by 42%; 57 full-time and 28 part-time
employees were made redundant in 2010.

Next to that, Deseret Digital, a new organisation, was set up
to take full advantage of the higher-volume, lower-margin
opportunities offered by the Internet (Transformation B).
The idea was to create tomorrow's growth by focusing on new
customers' needs and learning how to address them.

By combining in-house produced pieces with crowdsourced material from external contributors, Deseret Digital could produce content at a fraction of the traditional price. The digital offerings focused on the same subjects that had built the paper's reputation, but in ways that had no analogue in print. In addition to online news content, Deseret Digital developed new products, such as a media guide to which readers contributed movie appraisals, generating revenue through syndication.

To enable this future growth engine, Deseret created a "resource exchange", a new capability that allowed the two transformation efforts to share sources without interfering with each other's operations. The two transformations would be operated *distinctly but still be linked*. The idea was that by sharing these content resources with the core, the new business could gain a competitive advantage over independent startups. Deseret News and Deseret Digital shared a brand, editorial content, marketing resources and data about customers and their reading behaviour.

From 2008 to 2012, the combined daily and weekly print circulation doubled, generating enough ad revenue to turn the Deseret News into one of the country's fastest-growing print newspapers. From 2010 to 2014, Deseret Digital's growth rate was around 30%. By 2012, digital revenues accounted for a quarter of total corporate revenues, and by the end of 2014, their share had grown to 33%. More than 50% of Deseret Digital's revenues came from non-display formats (i.e. classifieds, deals, travel bookings, business listings). Non-display revenues continued to grow, keeping Deseret Digital's growth rate in the double digits.

Deseret's dual transformation approach illustrates how clean breaks with the past are not the only viable option to deal with digital disruption, despite its significant impact on the legacy business. Not only is it impractical, but it is also often not desirable to throw out the baby with the bathwater. At Deseret, it was the smart combination of Transformations A and B that allowed them to survive. They successfully transformed the core, granting the new digital growth business time to establish itself, without, however, completely decoupling the two businesses.

What's your digital operating model

You will need to strategise about the relationship between the digital growth options in your portfolio: Will options share customer and product data, and if so, under which conditions? Will they have shared digital platform choices? Will they share key partners? What about sharing data resources in external partnerships? Etc.

The set of critical digital *resource sharing* (i.e. leveraging) choices that define the relationship (i.e. dependencies) between the digital growth options in your portfolio at a strategic level is referred to as your digital operating model. Your choice of operating model determines the level of decision discretion awarded to the management of each of the options.

A useful lens for established organisations that want to strategise about new digital growth options and their relationship to the current core is the "forget, borrow and learn" model by Vijay

Govindarajan and Chris Trimble.[20] The idea is that with every new growth option, you need to decide how its business model (i.e. the way it creates and captures value) will be connected to the current core business:

- Which strategic assumptions of the existing core business must this growth option forget to win?
- Which resources must this growth option borrow (i.e. share/leverage) from the current core business?
- What must this growth option learn, or be allowed to learn, to win in its uncertain new market?

"Strategic experiments" are given special attention by Govindarajan and Trimble. These high-growth-potential new businesses that test the viability of unproven business models involve both forgetting and borrowing (see Figure 2). Deseret Digital serves as a case in point for this *distinct but still linked* digital growth strategy. Crucial to its success was the "resource exchange" Deseret News created that allowed its core transformation (i.e. "Transformation A") and Deseret Digital (i.e. "Transformation B"), a new organisation, to share sources without interfering with each other's operations.

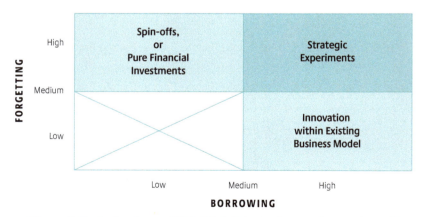

Figure 2. Govindarajan and Trimble's "strategic experiments" combine borrowing and forgetting[21]

In general, forgetting and borrowing is a difficult combination to achieve. Borrowing from the current core aims at accelerating the growth of the new option. But borrowing inevitably means coordinating and influencing which, if not lightweight enough, jeopardises the need for the new growth option to also forget. Forgetting will be essential for exploring new customers' needs, and to learn how to solve their problems.

That paradoxical nature of strategic experiments makes them challenging to manage. It makes them difficult to assign to either of the extend or self-disrupt portfolio compartments as well. Indeed, on the one hand, they target non-linear shifts in business models. But on the other hand, they also operate against the popular advice of keeping more radical or revolutionary business model innovations as far from the core as possible. They are distinct but remain linked. Luckily, Govindarajan and Trimble's book, *Ten Rules for Strategic Innovators*,[22] offers practical advice to increase the odds of success. For example, it advocates choosing for a radical departure from existing business, testing an unproven business model, focusing on high revenue growth potential, and, of course, borrowing existing strengths.

Architecting your way into new growth

Releasing digital resources through APIs enables you to leverage them as building blocks across different internal and external growth options in more loosely coupled ways than ever before.
Indeed, thanks to technological developments and complementary advances in software engineering practice, digital resources can, in principle, be reused and combined with others more quickly, conveniently and efficiently than before. With this, the number of potentially interesting leveraged digital growth options increases exponentially. That is, you can fully exploit the pattern of combinatorial digital innovation.

However, just because growth options can share digital resources with other growth options, does not mean that the value of sharing exceeds the cost. The tension between borrowing and forgetting across different growth options always needs to be anticipated and carefully pondered. Despite modern digital developments, coordination (i.e. governance) costs between options that want to share resources may be deceptively high, especially when involving external partners.

So, out of a multitude of possible leveraged digital growth options, which ones are actually worthwhile pursuing? You won't know until you have a good view of your digital resource architecture. Which digital resources can you leverage at an acceptable cost? To answer that question, you need to know the cost of making the resources into reusable building blocks in contexts that are different from the ones in which the resources originated. If your digital resource architecture looks like spaghetti, leveraging resources can be a very costly affair.

For example, that is why KPN's strategic decision to architect its way into new digital growth was critical for making its transformation successful. Bouke Hoving, chief information officer at KPN:[23]

"By agreeing to that [architectural] picture top-down, the board gave us a full mandate to execute a fast, 'no-compromise' transformation. It was a very bold choice. We needed to proceed quickly and did not have an all-encompassing plan for change, but we had this clear view of where we were heading. We always had great architects at KPN, but in the past, we had not listened very carefully. By giving back the mental mandate, we created totally different conversations."

CONCLUSION

What is the essence of creating a vigilant strategic routine for digital transformation? Kick it off by growing a profound appreciation for the new digital realities that are out there driving business success. Envision an ambitious point of view of the organisation as it succeeds in the digital age. Give yourself a strong sense of purpose. Develop a matching growth portfolio of real digital options for alternative future scenarios. Make investment course corrections as regularly as required by using actual feedback and by continuously monitoring uncertainties in the environment. Consider options for strengthening and extending the core as well as options for self-disruption. Carefully evaluate your digital operating model choices in the process of strategising about transformation and future growth.

Business strategy continues to be about making tough choices, about deciding where and how to allocate scarce resources. Today, the best companies make the cycle of challenging their strategy from the outside-in go faster. They aim to remain in sync with the rate of change on the outside: Taking options when the opportunity arises, lifting and scaling the best ones quickly, anticipating or countering possible threats, killing early, options that prove no longer interesting, even though the latter may be particularly difficult. They make strategic vigilance part of their resource allocation routine.

GREAT CUSTOMER EXPERIENCE EMERGES FROM THE WAY YOU SOLVE YOUR CUSTOMERS' PROBLEMS

2

DIGITAL REALITY NO. 1: CUSTOMER EXPERIENCE IS VALUE

The digital economy has put customers firmly in the driving seat. Freely roaming around the Internet, triggered by popups or alerts and assisted by digital voice assistants, customers are switching between different sites, between their laptops and their mobile apps, combining online searching with offline buying and vice versa. The boundaries between online and offline are increasingly blurred. Customers want, and digital technology allows them to take control of their lives' journeys. Smart companies capitalise on this insight.

If you've got some money in your wallet looking for a home, check out Motif Investing, an online broker, but not just any one. Motif promises to make investing hassle-free, low-cost, but at the same time meaningful, and even fun. You can translate your own insights, preferences and values into your personal basket of stocks and funds (called "motif"), with just a few clicks. Users can create their own motifs, invest in motifs built by Motif, or invest in motifs built by other users of the platform. Prefer to "shop after you drop"? Invest in a motif called "Couch Commerce",[1] composed of e-commerce shopping stocks. The "Rest In Peace"[2] motif lets you invest in the death care industry, with "customers you can count on". As Benjamin Franklin once said:[3] "In this world nothing can be said to be certain, except death and taxes."

Motif uses digital advances to co-create investments that inspire its customers, like clean technology, biotechnology or cybersecurity, conveniently and efficiently, from their smartphones, wherever and whenever the desire hits them. By deploying robo-advisors[4] maximally, Motif pushes process automation to its limits to create a unique combination of customer convenience and flexibility. More than the product, the customers are enjoying the experience itself; an idea coined by Motif investing in its original tagline:[5] "Stop picking stocks, start picking ideas."

This example illustrates how products and services are no longer enough to win over or keep customers in the digital era. The digital space is notorious for how fast it commoditises products and services. Ultimately, value is attributed to the total experience of engaging with customers in ways that fit with their connected mobile and social lives. Making your organisation's digital transformation work, will require a radical shift from taking an inside-out, company-centric product perspective to taking an outside-in, customer-centric experience perspective for creating customer value.

Access and convenience as new normal

Some 20 years ago, inspired by the rise of the Internet, Joseph Pine and James Gilmore oracled the arrival of the "experience economy".[6] Experiences, they argued, are a source of economic value, just like commodities, products and services, but they are distinctly different. Experiences are positioned as the next step in a historical progression of the definition of value. Experiences are personal, intense – especially in consumer businesses – and represent a customer response that says: "You absolutely get me!"

Many companies did not see it then. Now, we have Uber, Airbnb and Lending Club, for example, to highlight the profound impact of democratised access to digital technologies on customer expectations. These companies illustrate a broader digitalisation phenomenon that is setting a new normal for customer value based on ease of access, convenience and cost-efficiency beyond anything pre-digital companies can offer.

But are these dimensions of value what makes up digital customer experience? Not quite. Granted, in most industries, the amount of transactional friction that digital allows us to cut is massive, and so are the customer value improvement opportunities. However, thanks to digital disruptors, convenience, access and cost are rapidly becoming hygiene factors, rather than true delighters. Although important as a competitive necessity, these value dimensions *per se* should not be mistaken for what makes a product or service into a truly valuable customer experience.

Uber is a thankful example to drive home a most essential observation linked to digitalisation and the nature of customer value creation: Customers no longer have to buy cars, they can now enjoy mobility. The same holds for your customers: They don't want to buy a product or a service; they need "a job to be done". This job to be done reasoning was presented by Clayton Christensen and Michael Raynor in *The Innovator's Solution*[7] as a framework for understanding what really motivates customers to make buying decisions. The idea is that when customers buy a product or service, they actually "hire" it to help them to do a "job" they need to get done.

The job to be done framework invites you to ask what your customer seeks to accomplish by buying from you. It helps you figure out the customer's true objective, i.e. "the progress that the customer is trying to make in a given circumstance – what the customer hopes to accomplish".[8] Once you get this, you will want to design great new customer experiences rooted in a unique interplay between the digital and the physical. You will understand you'll have to turn around the way you design, deliver and capture customer value. That means thinking differently, like a designer.

Accessing experience through design thinking

The connection between product innovation and designer methods goes a long way back. With the focus now more than ever on creating great customer experiences rather than just products and services, design has penetrated the core of the business. "Think like a designer" has become a buzz phrase not just in Silicon Valley but all over the digital world.

Global design company IDEO is widely acknowledged for having popularised design thinking. Former IDEO chief executive officer Tim Brown described design thinking as "a discipline that uses the designer's sensibility and methods to match people's needs with what is technologically feasible and what a viable business strategy can convert into customer value and market opportunity".[9]

Design thinking can best be portrayed as a principle-based problem-solving discipline that forces businesses to fundamentally rethink the customers' jobs to be done, value propositions and the nature of work. Its principles pertain to the way customer value is defined as well as the way problems are solved. There is one underlying meta-principle, which design thinking shares with other "agile" frameworks and methodologies: The acceptance that the world we live in is not static or linear, but rather is a complex and dynamic system. Instead of shying away from that turbulent environment, design thinkers embrace it in an ambition to create richer and more fitting customer solutions.[10]

Principle 1: Empathise

The empathy principle is the hallmark of design thinking. It states that great design is rooted in an empathic, rich, holistic understanding of human needs. Design thinkers refrain from jumping to solutions. They first spend ample time and effort to absorb the world as the customer would. They open themselves up to the whole person and try to unfold the complexities of a customer's emotions and desires (i.e. the heart), intentions (i.e. the head), and behaviours (i.e. the hands) in the context of a particular job to be done.

Design thinkers acquire a profound appreciation for the specific context in which a particular customer need appears. A popular template for painting that context is the customer (experience) journey map.[11] This diagram depicts the stages or steps that occur as a customer pursues a specific objective(s), and documents the experiences the customer goes through when interacting or engaging with a company or product, from the customer's point of view. See Figure 3, for an example.

	Objectives, scope, journey type				Customer segment / persona			
Moments of truth			♡		♡			♡
Key journey steps	AWARENESS	EVALUATION		PURCHASE		USE		AFTER-CARE
	Step	...	Step	...	Step	...	Step	...	Step	...
Actions, triggers, reactions, decisions, feelings, observations, thoughts								
Touchpoints / channels								
Performance	☹ ☺		☺	☹ ☺		☺		☹

Figure 3. Example customer journey map template[12]

Principle 2: Show it

Design thinkers resort to visual thinking to gain access to the experience space. Visual models such as customer journey maps allow them to involve a diversity of stakeholders in holistic, multi-faceted problem solving, capture the full richness of situations and experiences, and tell appealing stories. Concept tests and prototypes are promoted to show value early, and often, during the design process.

Most importantly, design thinkers operationalise the concept of customer experience as the customers' reaction to what they see, what they feel, what they sense and interpret when being exposed to (a model of) the value design at work. Design thinkers seek feedback – rather than appreciation, which makes design thinking co-creative by default.

Principle 3: Create and capture

Design thinking is not about creating beautiful artefacts. Design thinkers aspire to develop solutions that represent value for the customer, but also allow a business to capture that value. The solutions design thinkers go after combine customer desirability, technical and organisational feasibility and business viability. At every stage of the problem-solving process, design thinkers work to produce value that satisfies these three performance dimensions. Typically, establishing the desirability of a solution takes precedence in the early stages of a design thinking exercise. It gets balanced out for feasibility and viability considerations in the later stages.

Alex Osterwalder and Yves Pigneur's "business model canvas"[13] is a one-page visual schematic that is widely used to broaden the perspective on value design to include both the business and customer perspective (see Figure 4). The canvas is designed around a customer value proposition(s). It allows you to concisely describe and challenge a business model's hypotheses about desirability (i.e. customer facing; right side of the canvas, including value propositions), feasibility (i.e. resource and activity related; left side of the canvas, including key partners) and viability (i.e. profit formula; bottom part of the canvas).

Figure 4. Articulating desirability, feasibility and viability hypotheses with Osterwalder and Pigneur's "business model canvas"[14]

Principle 4: Diverge and converge

Design thinkers rely on divergent thinking, followed by convergent thinking for both the problem and the solution phases of the problem-solving process. Divergent thinking is about opening up, creatively generating options, hypotheses and choices. Convergent thinking is about narrowing down, choosing options and hypotheses and making choices. For example, Figure 5 shows this problem-solving logic for the case of Stanford d.school's five-stage design thinking process.[15]

Empathy requires divergent thinking. Divergence promotes an open-minded, creative problem-solving culture. It invites taking perspectives that look at the whole customer experience and that are forward-looking. It also stimulates exploration beyond the traditional perimeter, recognising that in other fields they may already have addressed problems similar to yours. In many cases, it will be smarter to borrow or reuse than to reinvent.

However, scope creep and analysis paralysis are important risks of stimulating divergence in problem-solving. These issues can be addressed by deploying two process governance tactics: Firstly, impose a swift and steady, predictable pace on the diverge and converge sequences of the design thinking process; and secondly, put a cap on the available resources upfront, thereby minimising the possible loss (i.e. downside risk). These tactics keep the problem-solving process manageable and result-oriented.

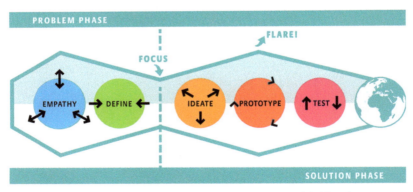

Figure 5. Sequencing divergent and convergent thinking for Stanford d.school's five-stage design thinking process[16]

Principle 5: Iterate and learn

Design thinkers may be ambitious and result-oriented; they also remain humble in their search for great solutions. For them, the world is too complex and dynamic to expect designs to be right first time. Indeed, it typically takes multiple iterations of problem and solution generation for all but the most uncomplicated problems to converge on a satisfactory solution. Moreover, the path to satisfaction may involve failure at any point, requiring designers to pick up the pieces and choose an alternative route. Failure is regarded as a natural part of the game, accepted, as long as it gets them closer to a result. When design thinkers fail, they fail smart.

Infusing critical thinking into a steadily paced progression of design iterations allows design thinkers to be smart: Staying focused and maximising the learning with every iteration. This objective is achieved by keeping designers conscious of the critical assumptions they make about what is a valuable solution. The process will ask them to make their crucial design choices explicit as hypotheses to be validated with customer feedback. The "experiment canvas" (see Figure 6), initially introduced by Ash Maurya as "the one-page experiment report" in his book *Scaling Lean*[17] is a useful instrument to facilitate this exercise (see Figure 6).

A "design pivot" is what will be required if a design's most important hypotheses are invalidated, which may happen at any moment in a turbulent environment. Pushing designers to be explicit about crucial design choices keeps them mindful of the biases they may have about what constitutes value. This way, value is not assumed but validated.

RISKIEST ASSUMPTION	RESULTS
What is the riskiest assumption you want to test?	Record the qualitative or quantitative results of the experiment
FALSIFIABLE HYPOTHESIS Construct your hypothesis	
We believe that < specific, testable action > _____	
Will drive < specific, measurable outcome > _____	**CONCLUSION** Did your results match your hypothesis? Or did they contradict your hypothesis? And was your result clear enough?
Within < timeframe > _____	
EXPERIMENT SETUP What kind of experiment will you use? What are you measuring? How many times?	☐ VALIDATED ☐ INVALIDATED ☐ INCONCLUSIVE
	NEXT STEPS What is your next move?

Figure 6. Breaking down assumptions using the "experiment canvas"[18]

Principle 6: Collaborate

It should be evident by now that design thinking requires different types of thinkers, stakeholders and disciplines to work closely together as a team to create desirable, feasible and viable customer experiences. Investing in boundary-spanning teamwork to gather all these different perspectives around a common process and principles is critical for design thinking to work. Just like design thinkers aim to empathise with their customer, team members will have to be able to understand, let in and trust one another.

Going for the digital edge in design

Digital technologies give a significant boost to design thinking. In their application lies a tremendous opportunity for enacting its principles of customer-centric value design. There are multiple interconnected angles to using digital technologies for rethinking customer experiences:

Automation: Streamlining customer journeys and business processes by connecting information digitally and eliminating wasteful manual labour, paperwork and complexity to make customer experiences easy, convenient and cost-effective.

> For example, reducing a complex payment process to a one-click payment; routing emails automatically by applying a set of business rules; and using blockchain[19] technology to eliminate costly middlemen.

Customisation/personalisation: Using information gathered from automation and other internal and external sources to customise or personalise experiences along customer journeys in real-time.

> For example, using a recommendation engine to suggest the best next movie based on a customer's preferences and behaviour; allowing kids to co-create their next Lego purchase using a toy design app; and using information generated by smart, connected energy grid substations to customise preventive asset-maintenance services.

Socialisation: Infusing social media information and adding social connectivity into customer journeys to enable or enrich customer experiences.

> For example, enabling job seekers to connect with trusted mentors in the sector of their dreams using Tinder-like swiping; allowing customers to vote for innovative ideas using a company's Facebook group; and using an immersive virtual reality environment to augment value co-creation with customers and partners.

Contextualisation: Using information pertaining to the digital and physical whereabouts of customers travelling along experience journeys to increase customer relevance and intimacy.

> For example, using intelligent second screen technology showing e-commerce opportunities detected from watched televised content in real-time; crowdsourcing real-time traffic information for suggesting the best alternative driving route at this or any later moment; and automatically adapting the format of a promotional message to a type of user device.

Design: Exploring the potential of using digital advances to benefit the design thinking process itself.

> For example, using rapid user interface mock-up apps to swiftly validate concepts; automating customer behaviour and satisfaction measurement; and deploying an artificial intelligence (AI) algorithm that learns how to improve experience design autonomously.

A fruitful way to help generate ideas to apply digital technologies for improving customer experience is targeting pain points in the customer journey where your customers are having a hard time. Special attention should go out to "moments of truth", i.e. key points in the journey where customers may pause and evaluate the experience, or make a crucial decision. Don't forget, however: It is the journey that eventually makes the difference, not an individual digital intervention or point solution. Always consider the impact on the customer journey as a whole.

What about agile development and Lean Startup?

However powerful its principles and process, design thinking by itself is unfortunately insufficient to cover all aspects of the idea-to-market process. It is therefore often combined with other agile frameworks and methodologies; with agile software development, devops and The Lean Startup chief among them. The latter take empathic design beyond prototypes to produce working software and create a successful business.

Agile software development: The *Agile Manifesto*, short for Manifesto for Agile Software Development, was written in February 2001 at a summit of seventeen independent-minded practitioners of several software development methodologies. It includes a formal proclamation of four key values and twelve principles to guide an iterative and people-centric approach to software development.[20] Its four key values are:

- Individuals and interactions are valued over processes and tools.
- Working software is valued over comprehensive documentation.
- Customer collaboration is valued over contract negotiation.
- Responding to change is valued over following a plan.[21]

Agile software development projects are often compared with traditional waterfall software development, which adheres to a formal, plan-based, sequential (i.e. non-iterative) software development process. Agile development projects, in contrast, take an iterative and incremental process approach.

Scrum,[22] for example, is one of the most popular process frameworks used for managing agile software development projects. Its use, however, extends beyond software development to the broader world of work. Unlike waterfall, but like other agile methodologies, scrum projects have a fixed schedule and resources, while the scope remains variable. The work is performed by autonomous, self-organising teams and planned in short, predictable cycles ("sprints"), aimed at continuous improvement. The team as a whole is responsible and accountable for producing a result with every sprint, at which time the customer gives feedback. Customer priorities are systematically reviewed and fed into the next sprint's work schedule.

Devops: What good is agile software development if at the end of a project the software is thrown over the wall to IT operations for maintenance? Especially in a world where customers are always on the move.

Devops is a clipped compound of development ("dev") and operations ("ops"). The term devops is used in several ways. In its broadest sense, it is used to refer to a cultural and professional movement that aims to break the historical wall between application development and IT operations through better communication and collaboration.

According to Gartner:[23]

> "Devops represents a change in IT culture, focusing on rapid IT service delivery through the adoption of agile, lean practices in the context of a system-oriented approach. Devops emphasises people (and culture), and it seeks to improve collaboration between operations and development teams. Devops implementations utilise technology – especially automation tools that can leverage an increasingly programmable and dynamic infrastructure from a life cycle perspective."[24]

Devops aims at establishing a culture and environment where building, testing, and releasing software can happen fast, frequently, and more reliably by using a strong bias towards automation. As such, "it is the next frontier in the evolution toward increasingly agile [software] development methodologies".[25]

The Lean Startup: Companies looking for inspiration to systematise the generation of new business growth opportunities often turn to Eric Ries' bestselling book, *The Lean Startup*.[26] From his early work with high-tech startups in Silicon Valley, Ries has created an entrepreneurial process for developing new businesses and products at increased speed-to-market. The Lean Startup combines hypothesis experimentation, iterative product releases and "customer-validated learning"[27] in a "build-measure-learn"[28] feedback loop.

Deep customer understanding guides this innovation process. That's where The Lean Startup and design thinking connect in practice: The empathy obtained from applying design thinking is used to generate crucial value hypotheses that are validated through a "minimum viable product" (MVP), i.e. "that version of the product which allows a team to collect the maximum amount of validated learning about customers with the minimum effort at a certain stage in the product development".[29]

We shouldn't forget, however, that Ries designed his methodology for a startup environment. That is, speed-to-market is not constrained by legacy culture, strategy, structure and operations. If, however, you're working for an established company that wants to adopt The Lean Startup's process, you'd better think through its desired connections to the standing organisation and the existing innovation processes, and reengineer these processes to accommodate the transformation challenge if necessary. The following questions can help you address the complexities:

- Will the new process replace existing innovation processes, and, if not, what will be their relationship?

- Will the new process share resources and support with the current business, and if so, how will this be organised?
- Will the output of the process be integrated into the current business, and if so, how will this happen?

Thinking more than skin deep

Many companies have made the mistake of creating apps – even very empathic ones – at the expense of consistent, integrated customer experience across channels, digital and physical. Some have created real app jungles, in which their customers, and employees, get completely lost. Others have activated all possible digital channels (websites, mobile apps, email, twitter, Facebook, etc.), but failed to recognise a customer as the same across these channels. That, of course, is not customer-centric. These inconsistencies quickly erode customer loyalty and brand.

The lesson? Don't confine customer experience design to organisational silos. If you want your customer focus to be effective and lasting, you need boundary-spanning coordination and collaboration across functions and channels. Great on-stage touchpoint engagement is built on the foundation of equally great behind-the-scenes business processes, i.e. end-to-end configurations of business activities that together create value for the customer. True customer-centricity requires taking a comprehensive organisational view, aligning incentives, business processes and structures.

This is where business process management (BPM) comes into play. BPM is the practical reference discipline for model-based development and improvement of an enterprise's work systems.[30] On the surface, BPM and digital transformation sound like a match made in heaven. Unfortunately, many don't see it that way. They'd rather avoid inviting BPM to the digital party, for several reasons.

First, past BPM initiatives all too often did not live up to their promises, for a number of reasons:

- They lost their focus on the customer.
- They emphasised cost cutting rather than customer improvements.
- They were confined to single departments or back-office processes rather than enterprise-wide.
- They focused on technology solutions rather than holistic work redesign.

Second, most BPM efforts were never designed to optimise business processes against the backdrop of a turbulent world, a business context that requires constant innovation and end-to-end agility. They targeted cost, efficiency and stability, rather than speed-to-market, flexibility and choice.

Third, in their attempts to make sense of the digital age, many existing organisations were blinded by what digital startups seemed to be doing. At first blush, they didn't seem to need BPM.

Successful companies, however, rely on a smart combination of customer-centricity and BPM. Amazon founder Jeff Bezos coined this idea into a famous success principle:[31] "We start with the customer and we work backward." Indeed, design thinking and customer journeys allow a company to start with the premise of being "customer-obsessed",[32] in Bezos' words. Adding a business process lens – in the case of Amazon applying lean process management principles[33] – allows them to subsequently work backwards to streamline experience creation end-to-end, as an activity process cutting through silos, beyond the line of visibility.

Successful companies digitalise customer journeys as well as business processes. But, they also digitalise their business processes in function of holistic, empathic customer experience. Business processes are reimagined for customers' jobs to be done and customers' journeys. The new realities of digital competition force the BPM discipline to enable agility as much as operational efficiency. That represents a serious challenge for BPM. Still, a challenge to be faced because, in digital transformation, there is a need for addressing business process change that cannot be dealt with by merely focusing on customer journey design.

A first critical requirement for BPM to reclaim its rightful position at the digital transformation table is to embrace design thinking principles. Two elements stand out on the technological side: Enabling convenient and consistent access to information across silos, for coordinating business activities end-to-end; and offering a capability to compose business processes on the spot, based on customer and business event data or analytics triggers. Not meeting these requirements, will make personalising customer experiences end-to-end a whole lot more complicated, impossible in real-time.

CONCLUSION

In today's turbulent world, competition revolves around
customer experience, a non-trivial value concept. Design
thinking offers a practical lens for acting your way into a
new way of "experience is value" thinking. If its application
stays confined to an organisational silo, however, the effect
will be marginal at best, but most likely counterproductive.
For digital transformation purposes, the advice is to connect
design thinking with BPM, understanding that establishing
this connection will very likely require the BPM discipline to
transform itself.

GIVING DATA
HANDS AND FEET
IS CRUCIAL
TO THE SUCCESS
OF A DIGITAL
TRANSFORMATION

3

HOW TO CATCH A MOVING TARGET

Successful companies understand that being relevant once is not enough. They must remain relevant and appealing, at the speed of the Internet, the speed at which their customers move. They do this by deploying data capabilities broadly, effectively stapling themselves to a customer's digital self. They bank on digital technologies to continuously monitor the environment. They sense customer needs and track behaviour in real-time and systematically run experiments to see what works and what doesn't. They treat value propositions as a set of critical assumptions to be continuously validated.

For such digitally attuned companies, the adoption of analytics for business decision making comes naturally. In their book *Competing on Analytics*[1] Thomas Davenport and Jeanne Harris refer to analytics as "the extensive use of data, statistical and quantitative analysis, exploratory and predictive models, and fact-based management to drive decisions and actions". Business analytics capabilities allow companies to move from being product-oriented to being able to offer a continuation of valuable customer experiences. They enable digital frontrunners to be effective at treating their customers as the moving targets they are.

Targeting reach and richness

Thanks to modern business analytics, we finally seem to be able to blow up the trade-off between "reach" (i.e. convincing more customers with a particular information-based proposition) and "richness" (i.e. reigning in customers with a more complex, customised or personalised information-based proposition) in the transfer of information.[2]

For a long time, the belief has been that IT couldn't achieve both: the greater the reach, the less rich the information offering and customer engagement, and vice-versa. Thus, digital channels targeting a mass audience were restricted to providing simple products and services, with standard transactions, requiring low-touch engagement. More complex customised or personalised transactions, on the other hand, required face-to-face channels and decision making based primarily on human engagement, possibly supported by customer relationship management tools.

Those days are over. Successful organisations now seek competitive advantage using analytics to break the trade-off between reach and richness.

MINI-CASE
ING competes against the reach-richness trade-off

ING banking Group has always profiled itself as a frontrunner in digital innovation in the financial sector. In 2014, it announced it wanted to lead anew:[3] "When we launched ING Direct in 1997, we changed the banking landscape. We were the disruptive challengers then and we need to disrupt again today." ING's Think Forward[4] strategy committed to make the bank excel with a promise to be clear and easy to engage with, help customers make smart financial decisions anytime, anywhere, empower them, and keep getting better for customers. Figure 7 summarises that strategy.

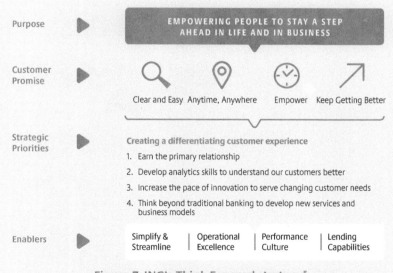

Figure 7. ING's Think Forward strategy[5]

In 2016, the Group's chief executive officer Ralph Hamers told investors that ING was going to accelerate Think Forward with an investment in digital transformation of 800 million euros for 2016-2021.[6] It was to speed up ING's grand plan of moving its diverse set of country banking models into one digital model that provides the best customer experience in each country.

Figure 8 illustrates how ING planned to morph its two traditional banking model clusters in Europe, i.e. the branch-based models for high cross-buy (i.e. richness) and the direct models for simpler products and transactions (i.e. reach), into one "direct first model with high cross-buy"[7] using digital advances to break the reach-richness trade-off.

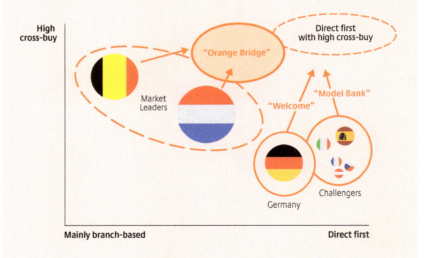

Figure 8. ING moving to one "direct first model with high cross-buy"[8]

With the extra investment, ING planned to build a globally scalable digital platform to cater for continued growth and improve the customer experience as it delivered new products quicker. The plans also included a significant investment in advanced analytics:[9] "We also see enormous potential in using robotics and artificial intelligence (AI) to improve accuracy, cycle time and productivity. Creating systems that can autonomously learn to perceive the world will allow us to address key challenges and provide personal assistance on a large scale."

Four types of analytics

Studies have pointed to the growing importance of business analytics, not only in analysing past performance but also in identifying opportunities to drive future performance.[10] The decision questions addressed by business analytics can be categorised in four types:[11]

- Descriptive analytics: What happened?
- Diagnostic analytics: Why did it happen?
- Predictive analytics: What will (i.e. is likely to) happen?
- Prescriptive analytics: What should I do?

The first two types of analytics are sometimes referred to as "business intelligence" (BI), the latter two as "advanced analytics".

These types of analytics questions are listed in order of increasing complexity of questioning entrusted to a machine. The sequence reflects a growing digital ambition, in the sense that the part of the decision process performed by a human decision-maker gets smaller as it is progressively replaced by machine intelligence, as depicted in Figure 9.

Inevitably, as data volumes are increasing and becoming more complex to use for fast cross-functional decision making, companies will have more difficulties to determine the most interesting and actionable findings. To keep up, they will need to transfer a more substantial part of the data-based decision making from humans to more sophisticated machines. The popular notion of "big data" was born out of the availability of advanced, cost-effective digital technologies and capabilities for handling high-volume, high-velocity and high-variety data. It gave what Davenport and Harris called "analytics competitors"[12] a significant boost: "[These companies use] analytics extensively and systematically to out-think and outexecute the competition."

Analytics competitors, essentially, compete on shortening four "analytics latencies" or delays (see Figure 9): "data latency" (i.e. the time needed to capture data and make them ready for analysis), "analysis latency" (i.e. the time needed to analyse the data and turn them into insights), "decision latency" (i.e. the time needed to use the insights to make decisions), and "action latency" (i.e. the time needed to put decisions into action).[13]

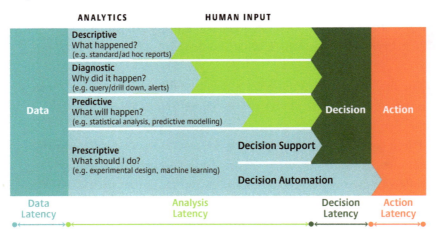

Figure 9. Four types of analytics questions and four analytics latencies[14]

In the years to come, prescriptive analytics will impact many jobs involving human decision making.[15] In some cases, machine intelligence will be used for "decision support", i.e. to augment human intelligence and contextual awareness. In other cases, it will be used for "decision automation", i.e. to allow machines to make decisions by themselves. For example, robotic trading has been a significant component of regulated equity markets for a while already: In 2012, Tabb Group estimated that it made up 51% of equity trades in the US and 39% in Europe.[16] Decision automation is now used in cars, factories, call centres, logistics (e.g. drones), to perform surgery, etc.

The next frontier for analytics competitors will be in driving up "analytics autonomy", i.e. "employ[ing] AI or cognitive technologies (such as machine learning) to create and improve [complex and dynamic decision] models and learn from data – all without human hypotheses and with substantially less involvement by human analysts".[17] Think of, for example, smart, connected vehicles that autonomously operate, enhance and personalise, that self-diagnose and service, and that self-coordinate their operation with other products or systems. Existing use cases include, but are not limited to, using autonomous robots in smart factories, smart, connected tractors in agriculture and autonomously operating mining equipment.

Building end-to-end data logistics

Too easily, business leaders are lured into believing that, because of their massive availability, data are not a problem. Experienced analytics professionals know better. For all of the excitement generated around the potential of analytics to transform businesses, turning data into customer and business value is often no small beer. There is more to this than just pushing and pulling data around.

In positioning yourself to benefit from new waves of technological opportunities, thinking in terms of end-to-end data logistics is practical.

End-to-end data logistics imply creating a systematic, high-performing process to gather data from a diverse set of sources, curate it for business analysis, and feed insights into decision processes in ways that lead to a desirable action. This process involves executing and coordinating a set of activities that together produce value for the customer and the business with an eye on the long term. Figure 10 provides a generic high-level logical view of a data logistics architecture for getting data in and getting analytics out. This architectural view allows you to treat data as an enterprise resource in its own right, managed to be broadly and conveniently used for creating customer and business value.

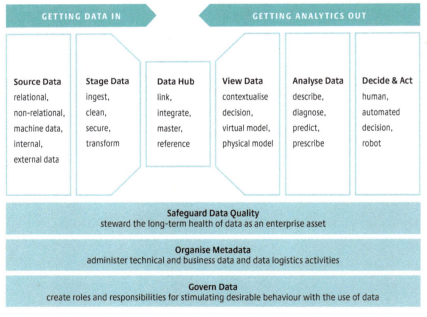

Figure 10. Generic high-level logical view of a data logistics architecture

The good news is that for each of the activities in Figure 10, advanced digital technologies are available for creating a competitive advantage. These technologies allow you to do things faster, cheaper and better than before. The bad news is that there is no one uniform technology capable of supporting the whole architecture or of dealing with every type of data and analytics job. Also, the technology space continues to evolve rapidly.

Moreover, unless you are a starting business, you probably also have some legacy data and analytics technologies. Luckily, in most cases, you won't have to replace all that legacy at once. Many of these "older technologies" still have a lot of potential and possibilities. So, rather than thinking in terms of replacing your entire legacy data logistics architecture, think about upgrading, selectively extending and renewing your legacy with new digital capabilities. Based on a firm understanding of your business strategy reimagined for the digital economy, map out your roadmap to adapt and mature your technology configuration in stages. You'll, of course, need professional IT architecture skills to implement your technology strategy properly.

Different data logistics for exploration and exploitation

While there are many possible data logistics architecture configurations, it makes sense to think differently about these data logistics for exploration and exploitation purposes. Data exploration environments should allow you to travel through unfamiliar areas to learn about them and discover new insights and opportunities. Data exploitation environments aim to make full use of the insights and productively capture the value from opportunities. For sure, big data technology advances expand the exploration possibilities. But many of the technologies are equally useful in exploitation settings. Essentially, exploration is not a product or a technology. It is a data logistics process.

Data exploration and exploitation environments carry distinctly different characteristics and requirements:

- Explorational use of data is characterised by freedom, openness, trial and error, generativity, advantages of scope, ad hoc activity, non-standard behaviour, bricolage. For example, you will want to play around with the latest (beta) versions of algorithms. You'll get your hands dirty with open source software and will want to share freely with colleagues and academics.
- Exploitational use of data is characterised by more control and mediated access, first-time-right, productivity, advantages of scale, agreed service levels, standardisation, industrial quality.

Each environment comes with different data quality, meta-data and data governance considerations. Successful companies manage to have adequate data logistics for exploration and for exploitation. Most importantly, however, they are also capable of smoothly transitioning initiatives from the *lighter-weight governance* necessary for exploration to the *heavier-weight governance* of the exploitation environment. To do so, however, requires excellent alignment between business, IT and analytics disciplines spanning both environments.

MINI-CASE
Enedis creates "fast IT"

In 2017, Enedis managed the public electricity distribution network for 95% of continental France. Its 38,000 employees oversaw the operation and development of 1.3 million km of power lines (42% of which were cables underground) and 750,000 transformers for 35 million retail customers. Enedis' network was one of the most reliable in the world. It ran on an annual investment in the order of 3 billion euros.[18]

In 2014, returning from an inspiring trip to Silicon Valley, Enedis' executive team initiated a digital transformation pro-gramme.[19] For the period 2015-2018, it earmarked 250 million euros for digital initiatives that would drive new operational efficiencies and customer innovations from Enedis' vast amount of data. The budget accounted for internal, external and technology resources. It did not include the 5 billion euros LINKY smart meter programme, which was well-established and functioned independently. Following a pilot involving more than 300,000 households, LINKY deployment started in late 2015 and was planned to continue until 2021, eventually serving over 90% of all retail customers.

As a first step, Enedis introduced three new teams – some 40 people in total, mostly internal transfers – charged with enabling digital transformation across the company: an innovation, an analytics and a data governance team. These teams soon joined forces to create a data environment that allowed mixed internal and external innovation teams to experiment with Enedis' data. The innovation team would design a fitting innovation process, the governance team would make sure the proper data usage rules were in place, and the analytics team would provide the data science support. The digital team issued an open invitation to innovate and collaborate internally and with external parties (e.g. startups and small and medium-sized enterprises).

One year into the programme, several successful data apps had come out. For example, one app gave real-time access to geographic data for those working in the field. Another one provided an operational cockpit showing network health indicators along with the status of healing actions. The executive team appreciated the progress that was being made. Still, discussions of whether the efforts effectively capitalised on the richness of Enedis' data revealed some areas that required special attention. One of them concerned the IT function.

The IT function was no stranger to data management. It had a long-standing investment in high-performance data processing for supporting the electricity network's operation. Fabrice Gourdellier, the chief information officer at Enedis, referred to that investment as "core IT". Governance for that data environment was extremely heavy, as even the slightest hiccup could bring the business, if not the whole electricity grid, down. However, what the digital team was asking, i.e. opening up Enedis' core data for convenient data exploration in real-time, was entirely new to the IT function. Jakob Harttung, the head of the innovation team:[20]

> "We couldn't do without the IT function. We had the innovation capacity; they had the scaling capabilities. But we needed a connection built around a kind of agility that they didn't have. So we caused friction. If there's no friction, there's no action."

Fabrice Gourdellier:[21]

> *"We were talking about 'fast IT' here. Development was speedy*
> *because developing the apps did not require changing our*
> *core production systems. We barely had to intervene. But on*
> *other occasions, we had to slow down, because the apps had*
> *security implications or required architectural or infrastructural*
> *intervention in our core IT [systems]. Then, we had to be more*
> *strict before allowing an app to go live. That's the trade-off between*
> *quality and speed. We simply could not allow jeopardising our*
> *[production] systems. Moreover, we were dealing with legacy issues."*

As a way to accommodate these issues, Gourdellier formalised
a distinction between fast and core IT. Both were considered
valid under certain circumstances. Fast IT worked towards
speedier and more flexible data exploration. It could be
used for digital product development that required minimal
intervention from the IT function. Innovators on the fast track
enjoyed lightweight data governance – designed so that the IT
function would not be a blocking factor for digital innovation.
"In principle, everyone could do it",[22] Gourdellier pledged.
However, from the moment projects required intervening
in the core IT systems, heavier governance would kick in –
although, here too, efforts were made to adopt more agility,
without jeopardising quality and security.

To grant even more development freedom while limiting the
risks, the IT function started delivering data and data services
through application programming interfaces (APIs). These
software interfaces – a combination of protocols, routines
and tools – were designed to offer self-service access without
requiring intervention by the IT function.

Data scientists aren't domain experts

When customers are moving at digital speed, customer experience creation and design thinking cannot do without advanced business analytics. The latter enable business experimentation and validation at a proper velocity. For example, principal research scientist Erik Brynjolfsson of the MIT Sloan Management School observed how leading companies capitalised on technology advances by simultaneously playing on four dimensions: measure, run experiments, share and replicate.[23]

An illustration involves using machine learning to run online experiments that continuously test website designs to optimise customer behaviour (e.g. time spent on a web page, click-through rate for advertisements, site navigation paths) without human analysts intervening. The advantage of this use of analytics, Brynjolfsson argues, is that "[it] can get at causality in a way that you can't with just pure measurement and [human] observation".[24]

Strategy and analytics experts Thomas Davenport and D.J. Patil have dubbed data scientist "the sexiest job of the 21st century".[25] The term "data science" signals how scientists, technologists, engineers, and mathematicians (STEM) have joined forces with data businesses to carve out their turf. Analytics competitors now benchmark against digital-savvy practices employed by highly-skilled advanced analytics professionals, who can make big money using science and technology advances (e.g. machine learning) to mine the gold in complex dynamic data.

But, in an interview with MIT Sloan Management Review, Digvijay Lamba, tech entrepreneur and former distinguished architect at Walmart Labs, speaks of a real issue with data science in practice:[26]

"What's happening is [that] there are domain experts – buyers, merchandisers, product managers and others [who] have worked in retail for years and years – these people know the market really well [...] They throw these ideas over the wall to data scientists, who go through the data and come up with these brilliant ideas to answer questions. But there is a wall there. The data scientists are not domain experts [...] What we want to do is break down the walls."

Some people like to paint a picture of the data scientist as a person with the curiosity to answer higher-order business questions combining STEM, hacking, data storytelling and business skills. Unfortunately, real-world data scientists aren't these superheroes with all the qualities and knowledge to make a data science project successful. Rarely are data scientists also domain experts.

To fully appreciate Lamba's challenge, it is useful to think about domain experts and data scientists experiencing the world in different ways.[27] Domain experts operate in the "business space". Their habitat is a space made up of real business transactions and interactions, and a large part of the knowledge they rely on has accumulated organically in the form of expertise and experience, which they apply in tacit ways. Data scientists must capture the business space in the "model space" in the form of concepts, models, measures, and hypotheses that they must test for their fit with the data (i.e. "modelling"). Any insight uncovered in the model space (i.e. "discovering") must then find its way back into the business space in a usable form (i.e. "operationalising") and be cultivated for optimal use (i.e. "cultivating"). This process is depicted in Figure 11.

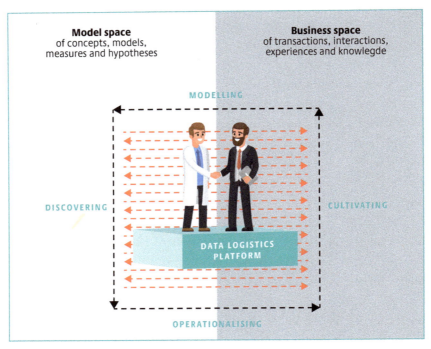

Model space
of concepts, models,
measures and hypotheses

Business space
of transactions, interactions,
experiences and knowlegde

MODELLING

DISCOVERING

CULTIVATING

DATA LOGISTICS
PLATFORM

OPERATIONALISING

Figure 11. Data scientists and domain experts collaborate across
the model and business spaces[28]

The real challenge of realising the benefits of data science, in practice, is enabling smooth transitions between the model and business spaces. And that proves hard to accomplish by just one person. It requires teamwork.

In the interview, Lamba mentioned that Walmart was building a "Social Genome Platform to drive unexpected insights – and close the gap between decision-makers and data scientists".[29] Indeed, connecting the business and the model spaces requires a robust data logistics platform for both data scientists and domain experts to stand on. However, traditionally, little if any attention has been paid to supporting collaboration with these platforms. This must be revisited: While data logistics platforms must enable data to flow seamlessly, they also need to promote conversation, collaboration and teamwork.

Enabling conversations and teamwork will stimulate the versatility of both domain experts and data scientists. With a proper platform, both will feel more confident and at ease to engage in the necessary boundary-spanning conversations. By facilitating this process of engaging, the platform will serve to create a common language and data and analytics culture.

Tips for running analytics projects

Applying design thinking significantly increases the chances of successfully managing business analytics projects. It helps to cater to the following success factors in managing analytics projects:[30]

Start with the end in mind: Business analytics projects are often characterised by uncertain or changing requirements (technological, functional, etc.). That makes managing a project's goals, scope and expectations particularly challenging. You may be in discovering mode, but remember, business analytics projects are not IT projects, nor pure data experiments. They are business projects, targeting customer and business objectives. Start with clarifying the objectives you aspire to, and then think about how you can most efficiently achieve those by applying analytics.

Plan, but plan for change: It is essential to plan, but do not overdo it. Have an execution bias, rather than a planning bias: Start with the assumption that the initial plan will have to change as the project progresses through iterations of validated learning. That is, aim for showing value early and often, and continuously try to capture the value of learning as you grow your minimum viable product (MVP) iteratively.

Take a holistic multi-disciplinary team view: Do you have business and data modelling, data discovery, operationalisation and cultivation skills seamlessly working together as a team all through a project's life? Do you have representation from business and IT for your analytics projects? Where are the data logistics people helping you to transition from exploration to exploitation? Your project teams must be able to manage the fruitful combination of business, analytics and IT to create desirable customer experiences with a viable business logic feasibly.

Work to gain stakeholder commitment: The lack of trust in advanced analytics remains a showstopper in substituting human work and decision making by computers.[31] This is especially true when using "black boxes", i.e. analytics with internal workings opaque to decision-makers like models created with AI. The black boxes, however, will be unavoidable as we move the analytics frontier forward. That means you'll have to work to develop trust in and gain adoption of machine solutions. Actively coaching the stakeholders into cultural change will be crucial.

Develop analytics capability project by project: Every business analytics project should be able to capitalise on the data products, insights, and lessons learned from previous projects. It also should serve as a springboard for next projects. You develop analytics capability over time, i.e. project by project. Ideally, every project's business case includes objectives for short-term business return as well as for long-term analytics capability development. Securing the long-term value of your data resources and analytics capabilities (including maintenance, improvement, reuse, etc.), requires data logistics, IT and other architectural disciplines to be involved in their development.

CONCLUSION

Successful companies strive to keep up with a customer's digital self. They want to capture this moving target effectively. They understand that using digital advances allows for forms of customer co-creation that cannot possibly be achieved with just human observation or design. It requires growing data and analytics prowess as an enterprise. Data scientists alone are not going to be enough. Business, analytics and IT have to join forces in creating an enterprise that thrives on smart data decisions. Don't underestimate the data logistics challenge. Project by project, you will have to grow your enterprise's analytics capability for exploring and exploiting opportunities more quickly than your competition.

COMBINATORIAL INNOVATION DRIVES DIGITAL PARTNERSHIPS, BUT THEY STILL MUST BE EARNED

4

DIGITAL PARTNERSHIP STRATEGIES REVEALED

Strategic partnerships are not new, but their importance has grown immensely in the digital economy. In 2017, McKinsey reported on interviewing 300 chief executive officers worldwide, across 37 sectors, about digital transformation.[1] One observation was that more than 30% of them had cross-industry dynamics top of mind. Many worried that companies from other industries had a clearer insight into their customers than they did.

Why not partner up? Digital partnerships are active collaborations between organisations aimed at capitalising on new digital opportunities. The reality is that no one company possesses all the data, digital skills and capabilities to win over today's demanding and dynamic customer. Competition is becoming a team sport. As digital innovation is essentially combinatorial, your innovation strength as an organisation will be limited by your ability to combine your digital resources with those of others.

Simply put: You bring your digital resources, I bring mine, and by combining them, we create great new value propositions and business models. Of course, it is never that simple, but that, essentially, is the digital opportunity out there. In other words, what will be vital for strategising about digital opportunities is going beyond the traditional analysis of knowing your customer and knowing your competition, to also getting to know your partners.

Adopting a partnership mindset

Going for partnerships as a strategic option for driving business growth implies adopting a certain mindset: A perspective you take on the relationship between you and other economic actors for creating and capturing value.

All suppliers will claim that they are your business partner. The truth is that only some are *partner-able*. For example, you may want to ask them how future-proof they think your business model is, and how they can make a difference. You'd be surprised (or maybe not) how many so-called partners will even fail to articulate your business model.

Partnering requires a focus on the other and shared objectives. The primary hypothesis is that you win together, and not just by yourself. Partnering implies thinking collaboration and co-creation instead of only transacting. It means aiming for long-term win-win scenarios, rather than short-term flings. Partners are willing to share the benefits of winning. They also commit to sharing efforts and risks.

A simple way to test the viability of a potential partnership is by drawing Table 1. Ask every partner to list the benefits they expect to get from the collaboration. Have them record also, the efforts they are willing to put in, the risks they are prepared to take to make the partnership a winning formula, and the conditions they require from the partnership. Sharing and communicating this information transparently will enable all involved parties to see at a glance whether a partnership can be made into an overall win, with every partner a net beneficiary.

	PARTNER 1	PARTNER 2	...	PARTNER n
Benefits expected	B_1	B_2	...	B_n
Efforts/costs put in	E_1	E_2	...	E_n
Risks taken	R_1	R_2	...	R_n
Conditions required	C_1	C_2	...	C_n

Table 1. Checking the viability of a business partnership

Table 1 also makes for an excellent partnership governance instrument. It helps to get a better sense of the costs involved in governing a partnership. These costs are incurred to make and keep the partnership healthy. In their work, *Strategy as Ecology*,[2] Marco Iansiti and Roy Levien identified three critical measures of "health" in business ecologies: "productivity" (i.e. the ability to consistently transform technology and other raw materials of innovation into lower costs and new products), "robustness" (i.e. the ability to survive disruptions such as unforeseen technological changes), and "meaningful diversity" (i.e. the ability to create valuable new functions or niches).

Partnership governance costs often stay under the radar, but need to be accounted for as well. In addition, it is wise to remember that although partnering can be highly productive, having more partners is not necessarily better, as the costs of governing a partnership tend to increase more than linearly with the number of partners involved. Of course, the best way to offset any (unexpected) partnership governance costs, is aiming at making the whole much larger than the sum of its parts.

Applying an ecosystem lens

In a digital world, where customer-centricity reigns and information flows at will, we need to broaden our view of competitors and opportunities. Thinking in "business ecosystems" offers a wide lens for identifying new opportunities to create and capture value, including digital partnerships.

Drawing on an analogy with biological ecosystems, leadership and strategy expert James F. Moore pioneered the concept of a business ecosystem for strategy in the 1990s.[3] He defined a business ecosystem as "an economic community supported by a foundation of interacting organisations and individuals – the organisms of the business world. The economic community produces goods and services of value to customers, who are themselves members of the ecosystem. The member organisms also include suppliers, lead producers, competitors, and other stakeholders. Over time, they co-evolve their capabilities and roles, and tend to align themselves with the directions set by one or more central companies. Those companies holding leadership roles[4] may change over time, but the function of ecosystem leader is valued by the community because it enables members to move toward shared visions to align their investments, and to find mutually supportive roles."[5]

Ecosystem mapping (i.e. conceptualisation and visualisation) is an indispensable tool to navigate your way through a business ecosystem. It keeps you focused. It keeps you from losing yourself in the complexities of applying a wide lens for strategy. Moreover, mapping is important to complete Table 1. That is why innovation and strategy expert Ron Adner of the Tuck School of Business and author of *The Wide Lens*[6] suggests mapping ecosystems with your partners:[7] "Making these [ecosystem] relationships clear […] forces everyone involved in the conversation to confront the challenges that lie beyond their own immediate responsibility."

An ecosystem mapping exercise starts with defining a focus, scope and boundaries. Specifying a "focal customer" and corresponding job to be done orients and scopes the mapping from the start. More importantly, it creates a focused, customer-centric view for strategy. The focal customer is the equivalent of the end-customer in a supply chain, i.e. a narrower lens representing a linear sequence of value exchanges (i.e. handovers) across different organisations from suppliers to producers to distributors to end-customers. With the focus, scope and boundaries clearly specified, the ecosystem and its dynamics can be made explicit by mapping the relevant actors (i.e. roles) and their value exchanges.

The process for ecosystem mapping goes as follows:[8]

Step 1: Define focus, scope and boundaries

Who is the focal customer of the ecosystem? What is that customer's job to be done? Analyse the driving and restraining forces in the competitive context around your focus (e.g. changes in economic, political, legal environments, evolving needs and preferences, social trends, technology developments). Make sure you start with setting a clear focus, scope and boundaries for the mapping exercise.

Step 2: Identify key actors

Identify the critical set of complementary and competitive actors or clusters of actors that directly or indirectly affect the focal customer within the defined context. Actors represent roles (e.g. lights producer, office worker, building owner), not particular individuals or companies. They are drawn as nodes in the map. Put the focal customer on the canvas first. Then map the other critical actors. Who are the actors representing existing supply chains that address the focal customer's job to be done? Use your competitive forces analysis to look broader: Who are the new, rising or potential key actors? Who are the key influencers?

Step 3: Draw value exchanges

Expose the value dynamics on the actor map by drawing the key value exchanges using directional arrows. That includes visualising both tangible and intangible value exchanges:[9] Which goods and services are exchanged? Where do money and credits change hands? Which important information do actors exchange? Which other intangible value (e.g. reputation, appreciation) is exchanged? One way to validate your mapping is by sequencing value exchanges along value paths to the focal customer that represent typical scenarios (e.g. existing supply chains).

Figure 12 illustrates mapping actors and value exchanges for a smart lighting ecosystem. The smart lighting context emerged from the use of digital technologies to make physical products (e.g. lamps, tubes, spots, strips) smart and connected. In their Harvard Business Review article "How Smart, Connected Products are Transforming Competition"[10] Michael Porter and James Heppelmann discuss new digital product capabilities, i.e. monitoring, control, optimisation and autonomy, and how they bring about a need for strategising across business ecosystems. In Figure 12, the focal customer is defined as a corporate office worker in a major city; the aspired job to be done as "brighten up the office and make life more convenient".

Step 4: Analyse collaborative and competitive dynamics

Complete your understanding by analysing the collaborative and competitive dynamics across the actor network. Who competes/ collaborates with whom? Who will or is likely to compete/ collaborate with whom? Who has or will have a dominant or leadership position?

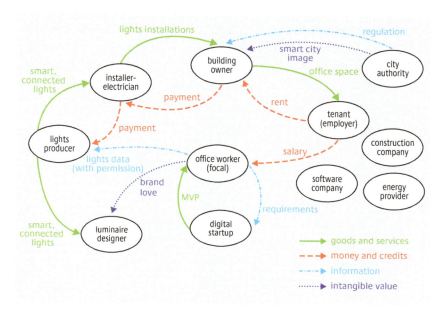

Figure 12. Mapping actors and value exchanges (incomplete) for a smart lighting ecosystem focused on a corporate office worker in a major city

With a good understanding of who the key actors are, which value they exchange and how the actor dynamics may play out in the future, you are well-equipped to identify, test and select alternative digital strategies. The analysis can reveal several options for strengthening or extending your current core, or self-disruption. Indeed, the ecosystem mapping analysis allows you to strategise about your role(s) and that of other actors for several new and existing value paths to a focal customer.[11]

Thanks to digital advances, new and more direct value paths to a focal customer are made possible. Existing paths can be made leaner, more adaptive and customer-centric; possibly by disintermediating other parties.

Any new or improved ecosystem value paths you decide to travel will likely require new or improved capabilities. You can decide to buy or build these capabilities. For example, consider Disney's acquisition of the major entertainment assets held by 20th Century Fox in March 2019.[12] Disney paid 71.3 billion US dollars to be able to create a more direct and integrated entertainment offering to the consumer. It chose to envelop all major roles in a vertical integration strategy to fend off competition from new digital competitors such as Netflix, Amazon Prime and Apple TV+ and older media giants such as Time Warner, Viacom and Comcast. Unfortunately, not all organisations have such deep pockets.

Instead of buying, like Disney, or building, which may take too long, you can also choose partners to accelerate your digital transformation.

Four digital partnership strategies

There are at least four digital partnership strategies for you to consider. That is, four types of digital partnership to create and capture value. The first one uses a supply chain lens for upgrading a B2B supplier relationship into a "business-for-business" (B4B) partnership. The other three partnership strategies take a wider business ecosystem lens.

Supplier-partners (B4B)

A first digital partnership strategy entails upgrading a B2B supplier relationship. Making the most out of the relationship requires the supplier to take a digital detour via its customer's customer.

Building on the smart lighting ecosystem example, consider the case of a lights producer with a simple supply chain that goes via installer-electricians to building owners. Once the lights are installed and powered up, office workers are able to enjoy the producer's products.

To avoid commoditisation, the producer decided to equip all its products with smart components (e.g. sensors, microprocessors, controls, data storage, software) and connectivity components (e.g. antennas, wired and wireless connection protocols). Our producer then designed a software to monitor the condition, operation and usage of light installations in real-time. Thanks to the software, installer-electricians can now sell seamless installation maintenance and repair services to their customers (i.e. building owners).

But that was just the start. Our producer, who used to be furthest removed from the end-customer in the supply chain, has now, thanks to its smart, connected products, a direct connection to office workers. And he also has access to digital product control, intelligence and autonomy capabilities.

Imagine all the things a smart, connected producer can do *as a supplier* for growing the business of installer-electricians. For example, our producer was fast in designing a convenient, customisable software app and a voice-controlled software assistant that let workers control office ambiance. Instead of selling light installations, installer-electricians can now sell smart lighting systems that increase the value of office buildings. Building owners love it, as it allows them to grow their tenant business. This digital supplier-partner case of a smart, connected lights producer is illustrated with the ecosystem map in Figure 13.

Digitally upgrading an existing B2B relationship to a supplier-partnership is a straightforward digital strategy for any supplier in any B2B context. A supplier will have to take a digital detour via its customer's customer. That is, use digital means to connect with the latter, and possibly connect with customers further down the supply chain. It will then feed the data and learnings flowing from this detour back into the original B2B relationship in the form of new offerings that are aimed at growing its customer's business. That's the B4B approach. The beauty of the case of the smart, connected lights producer is that with lights data systematically flowing back, the producer can create virtuous learning loops to fuel its partnership with installer-electricians on a continuous basis.

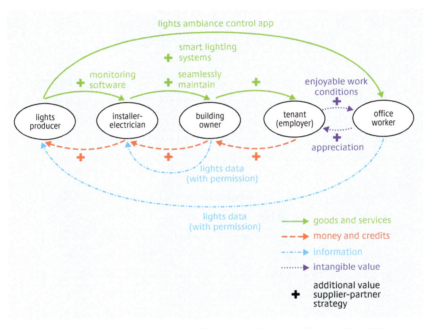

Figure 13. Mapping actors and value exchanges (incomplete) for the case of a smart, connected lights producer in a supplier-partner relationship with installer-electricians

Any supplier that successfully feeds the learnings from a digital detour via its customer's customer back into the original B2B relationship can earn significant partnership dividends. Pay-out will be in the form of increased customer loyalty, upselling opportunities and protected margins. The supplier will no longer be considered a mere supplier, but rather a digital partner. That, in turn, may open the door for other digital partnership opportunities.

Smart B2B customers will want to stimulate digital supplier-partnerships as part of their digital transformation. Both parties, however, will need to show trust and agree on a governance of their new relationship that eventually benefits both parties, instead of one. Otherwise, don't bother speaking about a partnership.

Collaborative innovation

A second partnership strategy involves two or more ecosystem parties bringing together complementary digital resources with the intent to collaboratively invent and commercialise new customer solutions.

Let's go back to our smart, connected lights case. Our lights producer decided to expand its digital growth portfolio by taking a minority stake in a selection of external startups that work on more radical lighting innovations. The investment is intended to help the startups bring their innovations faster to the market. However, the producer's motives for investing are more than just financial. It wants its investments to be of a strategic nature as well. That is why it chose to forego a purely financial investment strategy and go for a collaborative innovation strategy.

More than funding or keeping innovative startups close, the producer wants to actively engage by pooling ideas, leveraging data and other critical resources with a focus on a shared customer (e.g. office workers). To make that collaborative innovation idea real, the lights producer created a corporate digital accelerator for hosting its selection of external startups.[13]

The corporate digital accelerator is set up as a separate business unit. It selects and funds promising external startups, to which it offers shared, inspirational housing. It also assists in gaining access to company personnel and stakeholders, the startup scaling scene and external experts. It facilitates and mediates access to the producer's market, and to its smart lighting intellectual property (IP). The deal that is struck between the producer and the startups makes sense to both partners, and the spirit of partnership is carefully guarded. Our smart, connected lights producer's collaborative innovation setup is illustrated with the ecosystem map in Figure 14.

Let's look at a different example: Consulting companies such as McKinsey, Accenture and KPMG are also looking for collaborative innovation schemes to capitalise on new digital opportunities, not just *for*, but *with* their consulting clients. They offer to collaborate with the ambition to leverage their partners' digital resources for business model innovation. Essentially, they help companies engaged in digital transformation monetise their data and other valuable digital resources. Several deals may be negotiated that go beyond traditional consulting or getting paid for supplying advice. These deals include, but are not limited to, royalty arrangements for jointly developed intellectual property and launching digital joint ventures.

What all collaborative innovation partnerships have in common is that, in the spirit of partnership, the parties will want to organise their collaboration for the long term. That implies that they are willing to invest in managing their relationship as a partnership and in systematising the required resource exchanges across their organisational boundaries.

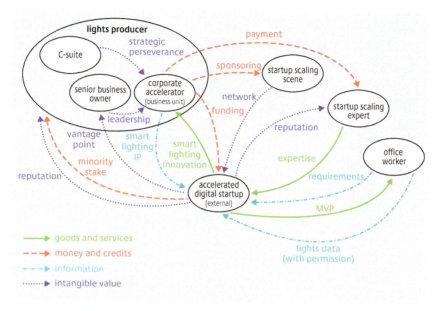

Figure 14. Mapping actors and value exchanges (incomplete) for the case of a smart, connected lights producer collaboratively innovating with external startups hosted in a corporate digital accelerator

Innovation component platforms

A third partnership strategy involves opening up one or more proprietary digital resources as building blocks (i.e. components) for easy reuse to external innovators. The building blocks are offered "as a platform", which signals that the intent is to provide the components in such a way that they provide a convenient, flexible and robust (i.e. trustworthy) foundation on top of which other parties can develop complementary digital innovations.

Think of a credit card company that makes available a proprietary credit rating service or an authentication service for practical reuse by external programmers, using application programming interfaces (APIs) packaged in an easy-to-use software development kit (SDK). These programmers can then efficiently integrate these services into, for example, mobile and social e-commerce offerings that they develop for their customers.

That is what financial services company Capital One is aiming for with its DevExchange[14] portal. Alongside access to a selection of APIs such as Bank Account Starter, Virtual Card Numbers and Identity Proofing, the portal offers several SDK capabilities that aim to make the lives of external software developers as easy as possible.[15] The platform's developer engagement features include self-service developer registration and instant API access, sandbox testing environments, documentation, code snippets, and reference applications with sample code.

The smart, connected lights producer from our previous examples could adopt a similar component platform strategy. Our producer currently offers its own apps for personalising light experiences, but why settle for the default when there are so many creative people out there? Why not give a broad set of software developers access to its smart, connected lights via APIs? That allows them to create even cooler new lighting apps. Think about developing a DJ setup app, or an app programmed to synchronise the producer's lights with compatible smart TVs and game consoles to create totally immersive light experiences. Figure 15 illustrates this case of a smart, connected lights producer selling as-a-platform access to its products through APIs.

Focusing on the other requires an innovation component platform to go beyond offering the development features for plug-and-play component reuse and convenient mashup with other digital component sources. It also needs to acquire enough knowledge about the type of innovator business(es) it aims to support; not too much, just enough to make its components useful to a range of external innovators. Only then will the platform gain real traction and be successful in creating a vibrant innovation ecosystem around the platform. For example, external innovators will expect that components by default comply with regulatory burdens that go with critical business use cases; that the platform offers compatibility with legacy systems; and that it attracts complementary component providers to increase the platform's value.

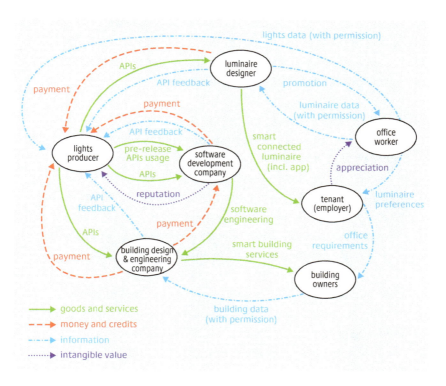

Figure 15. Mapping actors and value exchanges (incomplete) for the case of a smart, connected lights producer selling as-a-platform access to its products through APIs

By purposefully strategising to offer your selection of digital resources for external reuse, you can become a digital innovation partner of choice in one or more business ecosystems of your choosing. Pay-per-use or subscription models are straight monetisation options for your digital innovation component platform. However, more creative win-win value exchanges (involving money and credits, goods and services, information or other intangible value) between partners are perfectly thinkable.

Partnership platforms

A fourth way to exploit the digital partnership opportunity is by assuming the role of matchmaker for parties in search of digital partnerships. A partnership platform is intent on offering a convenient, flexible and robust foundation on top of which other parties can develop their digital partnerships.

In this scenario, you get paid for enabling digital partnerships. That is, for removing partnership governance costs such as partner search costs, contracting costs, co-creation costs and other frictions that might stand in the way of creating effective partnerships. As digital-savvy actors, partnership platforms will always be on the lookout for digital capabilities that help drive these frictions out. For example, you will want to investigate cases of using machine learning or blockchain technology to achieve that goal.

The actual services provided by a partnership platform depend on the type of partnership(s) it aims to enable and the extent to which it will facilitate partner relationships. For example, for our smart lighting ecosystem example, a partnership platform could be scoped to find digital startups collaborative innovation partners among lights producers and construction companies. This case is illustrated in Figure 16 with an ecosystem map. The platform could as well, for example, be scoped to enable more than partner search, involve more than lights producers and construction companies, and focus on more than smart office lighting innovations.

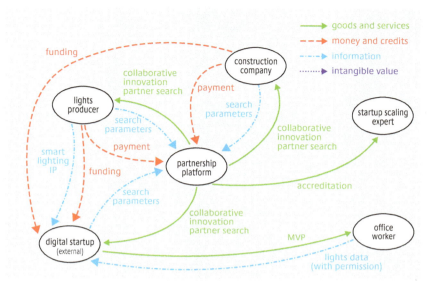

Figure 16. Mapping actors and value exchanges (incomplete) for the case of a partnership platform finding startups collaborative innovation partners among lights producers and construction companies

You may have heard of Techstars, a worldwide network that helps entrepreneurs succeed. It does so by acting as a partnership platform. Its origins lie in a deeply-rooted belief that community collaboration accelerates the pace of innovation. Since its inception in 2006, Techstars has developed matchmaking propositions ("programmes") for every stage of the entrepreneurial journey.

For example, Techstars Startup Weeks[16] were a five-day event formula aimed at connecting entrepreneurs, local leaders and friends around a local community's unique identity. As of 2019, local communities in over 300 cities were fed news as well by Techstars

Startup Digest,[17] an app "for all things startup in your community and around the world". Its content was curated by the community, for the community. Techstars also ran propositions for enabling more formal matchmaking opportunities, chief among which were its three-month "mentorship-driven accelerator programmes".[18]

Techstars brought together corporations ("member companies") and startup founders around certain themes through branded accelerator programmes. Global construction and engineering company Arcadis, for example, sponsored a City of 2030 Accelerator powered by Techstars.[19] Other accelerator programmes were supported by Techstars and more than one member company. For example, Music Accelerator[20] had Sony, Warner Music Group and eOne among its members.

Every year, after several months of global search, each accelerator programme selected the best ten theme-related startups. The average acceptance rate at Techstars was 1-2%.[21] Selected startups entered into an intense three-month growth acceleration journey with personal, hands-on mentorship, office space and a small cash infusion. In exchange, Techstars received common stock from the founders that participated in the programme. Following a three-month cycle, founders would meet with investors. By the end of 2019, Techstars managed about 50 accelerator programmes across more than 15 countries, and it counted over 1,900 alumni companies (86% active or acquired) with an average funding of 4.4 million US dollars per company.[22]

What is important for partnership platforms to remember, as well as for innovation component platforms, is that they are a foundation for others to build on, for partner ecosystems to thrive. Partners connect their fates to these platforms. That's why the responsibility for securing the health of the partner ecosystem naturally falls to them.

They will need to take a broad and forward-looking perspective on ecosystem health and be willing to make a significant investment in ecosystem governance with a view to stimulate long-term productivity, robustness and meaningful diversity.

CONCLUSION

Today, there are many digital partnership opportunities. Of course, there are also challenges. For example, you will have to learn how to use an ecosystem lens for strategising about digital partnerships. Plus, and most importantly, you will need good visibility on your organisation's digital resources to achieve any digital partnership ambition. In many organisations, these conditions for success are not obvious.

Arguably, the toughest challenge remains opening up to a partner. You'll have to feel comfortable with giving up some control. For example, you need to be okay with supplier-partners approaching your customers. Yet, these partners do not report to you in the way employees or business units do. You can't manage them in the same way. In other words, successful partnering requires a serious dose of trust, which needs to be created and maintained.

Good partnership governance will be crucial. However, designing and maintaining a partner engagement model that enables desirable partner behaviour and controls for unwanted behaviour, can be costly. The costs associated with bad governance or non-governance are most certainly higher, but may remain hidden for quite some time. Thankfully, effectively eliminating governance costs and enabling trust makes the business case for digital partnership platforms.

TECHNOLOGY SKILLS ARE AN ORGANISATION'S TICKET TO RIDE, AGILITY ITS TICKET TO HEAVEN

5

WHAT DIGITAL LEADERSHIP DOES

As Jack Welch, former chairman and chief executive officer of GE, once said:[1] "When the rate of change inside an institution becomes slower than the rate of change outside, the end is in sight. The only question is when." This quote nicely sums up the challenge that organisations face thanks to exponential changes caused by digitalisation.

Indeed, today's business leaders must ensure that their organisations possess the capacity to routinely explore and exploit opportunities faster than their rivals. That is, they must ensure organisational agility. That, of course, isn't easy.

So, how do you create the organisational agility required to succeed in the digital age? Well, you don't, at least not alone. But deploying the 4-V digital transformation leadership framework, synthesised from years of working with digital transformation practitioners and their organisations at Vlerick Business School, allows you to tackle this challenge with other leaders within your organisation.

4-V digital transformation leadership

The 4-V model (see Figure 17) uses two axes, four quadrants and four leadership types, i.e. the four Vs, to help you accomplish your goal of leading a digital transformation to achieve future-proof organisational agility.

Figure 17. 4-V leadership types enabling digital transformation

The vertical axis describes leadership as the ability to connect the dots for transforming an organisation: Ideas (i.e. mental representations) on the one hand, people (i.e. human agents) on the other. The horizontal axis represents the organisation's capacity to routinely explore and exploit opportunities *faster* than its rivals. Exploration identifies opportunities and assesses their potential, whereas exploitation (re)develops organisational capabilities to capture the value associated with interesting opportunities at scale. Today, exploration and exploitation must be reconceived for your organisation to thrive at digital speed.

Amid today's turbulence, leaders can't afford to take a back seat or delegate their organisations' digital transformation. That makes digital transformation leadership a matter of action. That is, leaders need to be actively involved in the transformation themselves, create a context for others to join the efforts in inventing new ways of working, and collaboratively learn and stimulate successful new work patterns to become routines. 4-V leaders own their organisation's digital transformation in a dual capacity: actor and designer. The synergistic interplay, the continuous feedback loop between these two capacities makes them agile leaders. Essentially, 4-V leaders are design thinkers: They act their way into new organisational thinking and design.

Making your digital transformation successful requires a combination of four types of leadership: Vigilant, Voyager, Visionary and Vested. These leadership types are *not* related to positions within your organisation, *nor* to personal style. Instead, they refer to four categories of behaviour (i.e. roles), advocated, role-modelled, designed into organisational practices[2] and stimulated in others by digital-savvy champions. That being said, a position can certainly be used for good. Organisations blessed with top and middle management wholeheartedly taking up their V-roles will have more luck in transforming their organisations into agile digital contenders.

Vigilant leader behaviour

It is not enough to have the courage and confidence to take a team out into new digital territories – in times of turbulence, vigilance is required. This means being always alert, curious and attentive to technology advances, changing customer behaviour, competitor moves, market disruptions and new entrants, and being ready to respond when necessary. Vigilant leaders are forever sharp-eyed, fascinated and circumspect. Their watchful demeanour allows their organisation to act quickly on the earliest, most feeble signs of opportunities or threats.

For example, one of the IT function's key responsibilities at ING Bank Slaski (Poland) was to make sure business leaders across the organisation were aware of emerging technology options. This allowed them to become digital leaders. So, IT systematically monitored the market for promising technology advances and startups and put them on a "radar". Chief information officer Miroslaw Forystek:[3]

> *"Our radar identifies trends and positions signals from outside. Using these data, we try to figure out, for example, what digital startups are doing. We combine data from multiple sources, including reports from companies like Gartner, Forrester, Boston Consulting Group and others, but also use input from meetings with our vendors and from scouting at events. We are aware that the vast amount of data sources cannot possibly all be scanned manually. That's why we are trying to use machine learning and data mining to help us filter and summarise."*

Senior management at ING used the radar practice to spot and assess threats and growth opportunities quarterly. The vigilant practice was designed to create awareness and inform ING decision-makers as well as to support strategic alignment.

More than data hoarders, digital leaders like Forystek and his colleagues in IT are data sense-makers. They enable organisations to make sense of what is happening beyond the periphery of the organisation, business model or industry, seeding idea generation with interesting perspectives, connecting weak signals and ideas and uncovering possibly underlying hypotheses or opportunities. They decode the turbulent environment for others by helping to build a common frame of reference for talking productively about what is out there. For example, proper framing avoids distractions and makes it easier for everyone to see interesting future world scenarios, agree on a focus and plan the collaborative transformation journey.

Most importantly, vigilant leaders understand that they must foster this observant, mindful behaviour in others. They lead by example, encouraging others to look outside the organisation and focus externally, stimulating exploration and external expeditions to develop strategic foresight and perception. Smart leaders don't wait for these reflexes to develop by accident – they purposefully create tools and practices that they embed into the organisational fabric.[4] They fully commit to using the power of readily available digital technologies to monitor, analyse, synthesise and share a wide array of data to stay current and identify business opportunities in a real-time world.

In short, to help their organisations succeed digitally, vigilant leaders

- remain always alert for new digital-age threats and opportunities beyond the periphery of their organisation or sector.
- make sense of the environment to enable others to identify and understand new digital opportunities and threats efficiently.
- inspire others to explore new ways of working, powered by digital technologies.
- look for digital technology to boost alertness throughout the organisation.

MINI-CASE
VIB scores with Tech Watch

*This mini-case serves as an illustration of how vigilant leadership can
be role-modelled and designed into practices that stimulate future-proof
organisational agility.*

At VIB, a Belgian non-profit life sciences research institute,
more than 1,500 scientists used advanced science and
technologies to study a wide variety of biological processes in
the human body, in plants and micro-organisms. The institute
had a standing track record in launching biotechnology
startups based on research developed by VIB scientists, and in
licencing VIB inventions to external companies. Its technology
vigilance practice – allowing the institute to spot breakthrough
biotechnology potential out there before the competitors do –
was core to its mission.[5]

Senior science policy manager Mark Veugelers planted the
seeds of the institute's digitalised technology vigilance practice,
Tech Watch, during his MBA in 2008 by exploring the
potential of using a variety of data mining techniques (e.g. text
mining, intelligent search, iterative clustering) to process data
from different sources.

A digital-savvy scientist himself, in the span of only a few
months, Veugelers managed to combine intelligence drawn from
academic literature data, patent data and data from the Internet
into a minimum viable decision-support tool to scout for breakthrough science and biotechnology world-wide. It was truly a
frugal experiment: Veugelers invested his own time and passion,

and he complemented the data and tools that VIB already had at its disposal with freely available open-source resources.

The next step for Veugelers involved transforming his ad hoc technology vigilance practice into a business process managed by a Tech Watch team. The process looked like this:[6]

- Using a broad, digital search strategy, the Tech Watch team scouts for technologies/companies of interest to VIB.
- The Tech Watch team informs VIB scientists or groups of interesting technologies/companies.
- A VIB scientist or group expresses interest in technology/company X.
- VIB contacts company X and explains Tech Watch.
- If company X shows interest – and with a convincing project proposal from the VIB scientist or group – Tech Watch awards "dating money" to the VIB scientist or group to try out company X's technology for generating scientific breakthroughs or new intellectual property (IP).

Tech Watch did more than keep VIB scientists alert. The vigilance was used to offer scientists dates with potentially interesting future partners. As of March 2017, VIB had invested in over 200 projects to test out the potential of newly emerging technologies through Tech Watch. Mark Veugelers:[7]

"An analysis of our investment portfolio showed the positive impact of our Tech Watch investments in terms of scientific breakthroughs and intellectual property. The return on investment (ROI) in technologies identified through our scouting outperforms the average ROI for VIB. Based on this evidence, VIB will continue to strengthen its vigilance practice to harvest value from early access to new breakthrough technologies."

Voyager leader behaviour

While vigilant leaders chart a map of the interesting unknown, it is up to the voyagers to take the first steps. Voyager leaders are the entrepreneurs who connect and team up people to make ideas tangible, bundling diversity and creativity to show opportunity at work. They take the abstract and make it real – inventing new ways of moving the business forward into a concrete mode of implementation. Today's voyagers do this faster, cheaper and better than their rivals by deploying digital collaboration and experimentation practices and tools that support a lean and agile business exploration process.

For example, Garry Lyons role-modelled and stimulated such voyager behaviour when he was the chief innovation officer at global payment solution provider MasterCard from May 2010 to June 2018. Lyons learned the trade when he was the chief executive officer of Orbiscom, a provider of innovative digital payment solutions to the global financial services industry, before its acquisition by MasterCard in 2008. He believed innovation should be science as much as art:[8]

> *"Business innovation can, and should, be a repeatable process. Like any science, you need robust methods and structured techniques to get results. Our MasterCard Labs are constantly inspired by what others do, how they innovate. We love to borrow good ideas, but we never simply copy approaches. We exercise discretion to make them fit the context of MasterCard without jeopardising their essence."*

MasterCard has been working hard for recognition as a premier digital innovator in global payments. It works towards becoming the digital foundation of a cashless society in which every device is a commercial device. MasterCard Labs,[9] a global network of digital innovation accelerator teams, plays a pivotal role in facilitating this ambition by taking an outside-in view and by committing to win-win digital partnerships between internal and external actors as its default innovation operating model.

Like MasterCard, many digital innovators have drawn inspiration from The Lean Startup[10] to structure their exploration of new products and businesses for increased speed-to-market. The Lean Startup process combines hypothesis experimentation, iterative product releases and customer-validated learning in a build-measure-learn feedback loop. Many have been equally inspired by design thinking (for customer-centric problem solving), agile software development (for best practices in software engineering), and other agile project frameworks and methodologies; all rooted in the premise that the world is a complex and dynamic place.

Indeed, voyager leaders don't assume that the way things have always been done is the best way to do them. They place a high value on learning and capturing lessons from experimentation. Data-driven decision making and learning by doing is built into the innovation process – with rapid, lean iterations between thinking and acting to discover what shows potential and what doesn't, progressively. The cycle of learning and unlearning is adopted, pragmatically, as an imperative. These leaders set out to explore the full potential of digital technologies to fuel that cycle by enabling better measurement, experimentation, information sharing and decision making.

In short, to help their organisations succeed digitally, voyager leaders

- **bundle together the diversity and creativity of individuals into an entrepreneurial team.**
- **explore solutions by efficiently progressing through a steadily-paced process of build–measure–learn feedback cycles.**

- use feedback from customers and other stakeholders to drive forward the exploration of solutions.
- look for digital technologies to boost the productivity of exploration teams.

MINI-CASE
VDAB goes for digital era government

This mini-case serves as an illustration of how voyager leadership can be role-modelled and designed into practices that stimulate future-proof organisational agility.

Government agencies are often depicted as being traditional, even conservative, organisations and laggards in the adoption of innovative technologies. Such was not the case for VDAB, the public employment services agency of Flanders (Belgium), which was forced to rethink its strategy in 2011 after being confronted with economic, political and financial challenges. Five years later, Fons Leroy, the chief executive officer at VDAB, and Paul Danneels, its chief information officer, had put the agency on a path to become a frontrunner for digital era government in Europe.[11]

VDAB created a New Digital Services Lab as part of its digital transformation to experiment with digital value propositions that matched job-seeking candidates more effectively with potential employers. The Lab served three purposes:

- Provide a safe zone for innovative digital experiments.
- Create a structured, efficient process for VDAB to innovate with digital technologies.

- Cultivate digital savviness and infuse new ways of working into the entire VDAB organisation.

The team in charge of the Lab was composed of a small group of people with different VDAB backgrounds. Niels Tanésy, the Lab manager:[12]

"I joined the Lab with experience as a team and project leader. I knew the business as well, but didn't have an IT background. At first, I was a bit surprised that Paul – our chief information officer – had offered me the job. But it made sense. The Lab was there to represent various views and stakeholders. This was about reinventing services for the labour market, not just about IT. For me, it was a great opportunity to grow professionally. I learned a lot about innovation, customer-centricity and data experiments."

To be able to take a fresh, outside-in look at public service innovation, the Lab operated outside of the day-to-day context of the existing organisation. Its way of working with projects was inspired by The Lean Startup and other agile development approaches. The Lab targeted new or under-served customer segments, such as students and immigrants, with digital servicing approaches that were different from the traditional, labour-intensive approach.

During its first year of operation, the Lab team developed a strategy of six simple rules to identify and select opportunities, dubbed "digital opportunity strategy", for public service innovation in the digital space.[13] The rules symbolised a clear break with critical operating choices of the past. They were intended to help the organisation, and its stakeholders better understand how VDAB must act differently in the future:

- *From* digital in support *to* digital-first.
- *From* stand-alone services *to* coordinated dynamic service journeys.
- *From* service provider *to* ecosystem orchestrator.
- *From* "have to" *to* "want to" partnerships.
- *From* plan-driven *to* agile projects.
- *From* ad hoc initiatives *to* developing organisational capabilities.

The Lab used these "boundary-breaking rules" to determine which digital initiatives would contribute to maximising value for new customer segments and to learning how to solve their problems.

One-week boot camp challenges served to filter ideas and prep those involved before entering the Lab. Once an idea made it into the Lab, it was developed using a build-measure-learn feedback loop. Projects in the Lab were regularly screened to determine whether they would continue to live in the Lab, move out into exploitation development for integration in the existing VDAB organisation, spun-off or be stopped.

Aside from providing the context for digital experimentation and coaching project teams during their stay in the Lab, team members invested much time growing a coalition of digital innovation ambassadors across VDAB. They went around with an open invitation to all employees by giving presentations, setting up sparring meetings, hosting pitching sessions, organising innovation boot camps, etc.

Visionary leader behaviour

Just like vigilant leaders, visionary leaders make sense of things. Vigilant leaders are skilled at framing *what is*. Visionary leaders welcome their vigilance as inspiration. They imagine *what could be*, and then paint a picture of the organisation's *to be* state (i.e. *what should be*), from a strategic point of view.

Visionary leaders have a unique ability to combine weak signals, ideas and experiments with great imagination and foresight into a winning business aspiration. Great visionaries tell an engaging and energising story of the organisation as it succeeds in the digital age. Their stories bring shared focus and commitment to the organisation, advocating the adoption of digital technologies to attain a competitive edge and capture business value at scale.

That is what Marc Benioff did when he looked at cloud computing early on and envisioned a grand opportunity for his new company, Salesforce.com, to reinvent the enterprise software business "as a service".[14] That's what agriculture equipment manufacturer John Deere did with its vision for smart, connected machines to revolutionise farming.[15] That's what Sreenath Sreenivasan, the chief digital officer at the New York Metropolitan Museum of Art (the Met) from June 2013 to August 2016, did when he coined the Met's aspiration to "tell a million-plus stories about a million-plus pieces of art to a billion-plus people",[16] by creating a virtuous circle between the online and offline visitor experience. The Met's goal was to create an online experience that was so compelling that people from all around the globe would put a visit on their bucket list.

Having an inspirational, forward-looking digital transformation story is a competitive resource in itself. It makes a critical difference in the war for digital talent. Talent should always be a strategic priority.

But having a story isn't enough. The scarce digital talent you want to attract, develop and hold so dearly, will soon figure out what sits beneath the marketing pitch. Visionary leaders won't neglect to translate the organisation's strategic intent into resource allocation choices that focus on creating new and improved core organisational capabilities. They'll ask: What does our organisation need to do really well, better than others, in this new digital economy to succeed with its customers?

One way to challenge your organisation's current core capabilities is to use job to be done[17] questioning at the highest level. Ask yourself what your digital-age customers really hope to accomplish by buying from you? What progress are they trying to make in a specific circumstance? You may be surprised (or not) how badly some of your current core organisational capabilities align with the jobs to be done for your increasingly digital-savvy customers.

Business strategies for the digital age will have to include a point of view on sharing digital resources across a strategic growth portfolio with options for strengthening the core, extending the core, and self-disruption. It would be wise to interrogate each strategic option for its core capabilities. Depending on this analysis, well-pondered strategic resource sharing decisions can be made. It will give rise to your digital operating model.

Today's visionary leaders also choose to compete with an ecosystem lens. They understand the innovation potential associated with digital partnerships. In digital ecosystems, partners successfully co-create and share value captured from combining resources in new, digital ways. Partners are not selected just to get easy and cost-effective access to resources, but rather to accelerate learning cycles through collaboration and co-creation, and to grow an economic pie together as a strategy.

For example, collaboration has always been at the heart of the UK capital's Smart London Plan,[18] i.e. "a long-term commitment to using the creative power of new technologies to serve London and improve Londoners' lives. [...] This effort will require new forms of collaboration between Londoners, government, businesses and academia to approach London's challenges in an ever more integrated way."

A pivotal strategic initiative, recognising the increasingly vital role that data sharing plays in supporting sustainable city development, is London Datastore,[19] the city's open and free data portal (i.e. a digital component innovation platform). Since its inception in 2010, hundreds of apps have been created by a variety of parties using the trend-setting portal. The broader Data for London Strategy,[20] underpinning the Datastore, aims "for London to have the most dynamic and productive City Data Market in the world". It commits to making all users of the data platform winners.

In short, to help their organisations succeed digitally, visionary leaders

- bring strategic intent to the organisation by telling an engaging and energising story of the organisation as it succeeds in the digital age.
- rethink the organisation's core organisational capabilities for achieving digital-age customer-centricity.
- envision success by combining the organisation's key digital resources and those of ecosystem partners.
- advocate the use of digital technologies to create competitive advantage.

MINI-CASE
Arcadis makes strategic sense of digital transformation

This mini-case serves as an illustration of how visionary leadership can be role-modelled and designed into practices that stimulate future-proof organisational agility.

The mission of Arcadis, a global design and consultancy company for natural and built assets, was as simple as it was compelling: "Improving quality of life." Arcadians all around the world designed and created places where citizens played, people learned, and communities lived.

For Arcadis, 2017 was a pivotal year. That year, Sidewalk Labs (a Google company) won a competition to build a high-tech Quayside neighbourhood in Toronto (Canada): Twelve acres of formerly industrial waterfront land would serve as a living laboratory for "reimagining cities from the Internet up".[21] This disruptive moment was a wake-up call for Arcadis. The company found itself confronted with competitors it had not even thought of as competitors.

The result? 27,000 Arcadians were invited on an accelerated digital transformation journey that would shift their thinking, skill sets and approaches. Peter Oosterveer, chief executive officer at Arcadis:[22] "In 2017, we set out to become a digital frontrunner in our industry by 2021." Employee surveys showed Arcadians desired to learn more and get busy with digital technologies. At the same time, there was confusion, doubt and insecurity: What did the digital frontrunner ambition actually mean?

Arcadis' designers and engineers had used building information modelling (BIM), i.e. an intelligent 3D model-based process, to more efficiently plan, design, construct and manage buildings and infrastructure for a while.[23] In other words, they created "digital twins" of physical assets. Weren't these professionals embracing digital transformation already? Did Arcadis' core BIM capability really need reinvention? Those questions kept BIM lead Bram Mommers busy.

Mommers led an informal scouting expedition in the second half of 2017, involving members of the newly formed Digital Office and of the local BIM teams, which brought more clarity. By confronting the current BIM practice with the new realities of digital competition it became clear that to become a digital frontrunner, Arcadis had to work towards a digital-age or "level 3" BIM vision.[24] The visual in Figure 18 helped to tell the story of the aspired digital transformation of the BIM practice; *from* supporting asset-centric *to* customer-centric design, and *from* enabling B2B *to* business ecosystem collaboration. It wasn't a complete view of what digital transformation entailed for Arcadis, but the BIM vision strengthened the case for radical action across Arcadis. It also gave rise to a broader business visioning exercise: Vision 2030.

With the kick-off of the Vision 2030 working group in early 2018, Arcadis sent a strong message that it wanted its digital transformation to be a collective and people-centric effort.

Figure 18. Towards a digital-age BIM capability[25]

Twenty-five Arcadians from across the globe, with different pro-
files and drawn from all levels in the organisation, were brought
together to embark on a visioning journey to reimagine Arcadis
improving quality of life in 2030. A consultancy was brought in to
facilitate a visioning process following design thinking principles.
Julien Cayet, the chief digital officer at Arcadis:[26]

> *"We selected a strategy consultant not to bring us a vision, but for
> their ability to allow our vision to emerge from the team's thinking.
> And that thinking needed to be outside-in, radical and together."*

The group sought information about issues and trends,
mustering inspiration from existing and potential stakeholders
and real-life observations. Using this input, they imagined
different scenarios of the future and possible roles, customer
propositions and business models for Arcadis. Six months on,
buy-in was sought at Arcadis' yearly Global Leadership Forum,
which also suggested ideas for fine-tuning. Vision 2030 ended
up giving rise to several cornerstones of Arcadis' new strategic

storyline; among them was a new vision statement:[27] "We improve quality of life by better understanding the human experience and connecting it with our scalable asset knowledge."

Arcadis' choice to adopt a human-centric perspective was also fundamental for redefining its strategic value focus. It redefined focus areas along the lines of thematic customer needs clusters (e.g. mobility, resilience and belonging) instead of engineering/design jobs (e.g. build roads and bridges), practices (e.g. project and programme management) or solutions (e.g. an analytical project budgeting application).

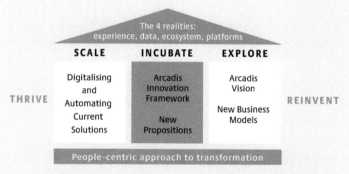

Figure 19. Arcadis' three compartments of growth for digital transformation[28]

Arcadis made its business aspiration of creating a new, digital blend between its proud legacy as an engineering company and human-centricity real by taking a portfolio view of investments in digital transformation along three growth compartments (see Figure 19): "Scale" (i.e. digitalising and automating current solutions), "Incubate" (i.e. developing new adjacent digital propositions) and "Explore" (i.e. fostering self-disruptive digital business models).

Vested leader behaviour

Vested leaders enable their organisations to move beyond experiments and visionary tales and steadily, progressively turn these into a productive, yet flexible, organisational machinery. Acting as true enterprise architects, they put the entire organisation, rather than individual pieces, on a roadmap to successful digital transformation. "Enterprise architecture" (EA) represents a logic for organising resources (e.g. skills, data, services, processes) into organisational capabilities. It reflects an operating model vision for the enterprise as a whole, as well as a process for working towards achieving that vision.[29]

Principal research scientist Jeanne Ross of the MIT Sloan Management School and her colleagues underscored the importance of using EA for competing as a digital business with their study of Nordstrom, a leading fashion specialty retailer.[30] Nordstrom's vision was to "integrate the store and online experience to enable customers to shop seamlessly any way they choose".[31] The researchers emphasised two essential success factors: The company's strong strategic focus and its architecting practice which enabled it to integrate new digital technologies in ways that empowered both employees and customers.

The Nordstrom case drives home an important point: Successful digital transformation is not so much about throwing out an old business or business model for a completely new one. Instead, it's about digitally strengthening the pieces that work and conveniently combining them with new digital opportunities. So, it falls to vested leaders to use architecture skills and practices to help the organisation as a whole develop a roadmap to create the new or improved winning organisational capabilities. At least as necessary, however, is that vested leadership facilitates and creates the right context for the organisational capability development itself.

In essence, vested leadership revolves around creating organisational mechanisms to swiftly mobilise skills and resources from a variety of disciplines and bring them together to plan, develop, improve and redevelop organisational capabilities. Vested leaders of the digital age are champions of crowdsourcing capability development, using a different concept of an organisation, which is focused much more on self-learning, teamwork and networking. They move away from the deeply embedded command-and-control organisation to design and promote an agile organisational architecture and culture.

For example, by 2016 dozens of agile-like organising experiments at various scales had popped up all over Dutch telecommunications company (telco) KPN.[32] Thus, the executive committee agreed that the company's digital transformation needed some unification in its agile work practices. The job of bringing alignment, coordination and integration to the agile grassroots initiatives fell to Lisette Oosterbroek, formerly responsible for new ways of working within KPN's digital programme, but now reporting directly to the chief executive officer. Oosterbroek had her views on how to achieve her objective:[33]

"I did not have a clear three-year, ten-step plan; which was difficult to sell to some of the top managers. I was not building a bridge. I believed in crossing the river by feeling the stones and being circumspect and pragmatic every step of the way. Like other early adopters within KPN, I had a dream for KPN to become this agile fleet of sailboats, navigating the oceans together. My view was to get there one stone at a time."

In 2017, this gave rise to KPN Kompas, a navigation guide for the organisation, its leaders, and employees. This guide was conceived not in isolation, but with and by a coalition of KPN employees who wished to work differently – and already did. Intent on providing direction and freedom, the document listed twelve guiding principles for thinking and working in agile ways. Kompas also proposed a unifying language for talking about agile organising. Inspired by the popular agile model in use at the digital music service Spotify, the guide spoke about issues such as organising in autonomous, multidisciplinary teams ("squads"), purposeful groupings of highly dependent teams ("tribes"), and cross team disciplinary development networks ("chapters").[34]

Vested leaders like Lisette Oosterbroek enable others to come together and achieve results. They transform complex organisations to create a context for empowered people to collaboratively develop and adopt new and improved work and organising practices, and to unlearn outdated practices. Today, this context is designed to promote customer- and results-orientation, self-organising teamwork and open knowledge flows within and among teams. It has *just enough* management structure to make productive adaptability thrive.

In short, to help their organisations succeed digitally, vested leaders

- put the entire organisation, rather than individual pieces, on a roadmap to successful digital transformation.
- mobilise the right skills and resources for timely exploration and exploitation of digital opportunities.
- make sure that new and existing resources can efficiently be reused for digital innovation.
- facilitate the development and adoption of successful digital technologies, work and organising practices across the organisation.

MINI-CASE
"Analytics as a Service" at UCB

This mini-case serves as an illustration of how vested leadership can be role-modelled and designed into practices that stimulate future-proof organisational agility.

Global biopharmaceutical company UCB developed innovative medicines and therapies for people living with severe diseases of the immune system or of the central nervous system, such as epilepsy or Parkinson's disease.

When Jean-Christophe Tellier became the chief executive officer of UCB in 2015, he launched a strategic shift from volume (i.e. selling more pills) to patient value creation (i.e. tailoring therapies for each patient, based on data about each patient, also known as "precision medicine").[35] One of the biggest challenges in tailoring therapies for each patient was building a holistic view of each patient from the many internal and external sources of data. Jean-Christophe Tellier:[36]

> *"I was fortunate to have Herman and his IT team on board. You sometimes need people who drive things simply through their curiosity — outside the strategy, outside the process, ahead of everyone else. Their passion for data and analytics was the foundation for many changes."*

Herman De Prins was UCB's chief information officer. Already in 2013, he and his team had launched an initiative labelled "Analytics as a Service" (AaaS). It was aimed at three objectives:

- Treating data as an organisational asset.
- Building internal analytics capabilities.
- Promoting a culture of innovating with data.

Though far from complete, the AaaS framework had been progressively implemented to support the enterprise since 2013.

Three enablers were introduced, making things real:

- Value Run: An agile data experimentation process coupled with a robust exploitation approach. Value runs aimed to stimulate business value-seeking behaviour with data (not undirected data exploration) and allow for fast learning and iterative and incremental insight-building.

- Data Lab: A sandbox environment for analytics teams to experiment with data. A data lab existed for a fixed period: Once the exploration was complete, the lab was decommissioned. The results (e.g. project descriptions, documentation, data and analytics products) were documented on Amplify.

- Amplify: A portal, meant to be the central point of reference for all analytics initiatives. It provided the latest news, served as an app store for data and analytics products (e.g. code, algorithms, analytics solutions), hosted data labs, and enabled knowledge management.

The idea was that these enablers should allow everyone at UCB to innovate patient value with data. Opportunities were everywhere: R&D (e.g. select better targets, reduce downstream failures), operations (e.g. minimise inventory, respond to unexpected events), and commercial (e.g. optimise the field force, create analytics-driven adherence).

To learn progressively and leverage insights collectively, a small central team was charged with continuously improving the AaaS enablers. They catered for the data logistics that supported the activities hosted on the Amplify platform. The team's mission was to build a productive analytics community that involved the whole of UCB. Their efforts in community-building focused on the following activities:

- Developing thought leadership (e.g. creating an analytics community of practice, scouting for interesting partnerships).
- Developing internal talent (e.g. setting up training curricula, offering fora and inspiration sessions).
- Promoting data-driven innovation (e.g. organising data science challenges, funding pioneer projects).

CONCLUSION

Digital transformation requires digital-savvy champions covering all four leadership types: Vigilant, Voyager, Visionary, and Vested. These role-models drive agility into the heads, hands and hearts of the organisation. They create tools and practices that they embed into the organisational fabric to achieve digital-age organisational agility. Without vigilant leaders, there's no sensing for relevance or giving sense to digital opportunities. Without voyager leaders, opportunities remain wild ideas or risky gambles at best. Without visionary leaders, there's no sense of digital purpose or focus on competing in the digital age. Without vested leaders, there's no architecting your way into becoming a flexible and adaptable digital highflier.

In successful organisations, each leadership type represents a social network or coalition of individuals spread across the organisation. The strength and interactions of these communities of practice[37] determine the success of the organisation's digital transformation.

The leadership types do not exist in isolation. They are intrinsically connected, interdependent. The real trick to digital transformation is to connect the leadership types virtuously. For example, when vested leaders develop a flexible architecture of loosely coupled, reusable digital resources, a whole world opens for voyager leaders to accelerate digital exploration projects. Voyager leaders will be more than happy to take advantage of this resource leveraging opportunity.

One individual can excel at more than one type of leadership behaviour. But excelling at all four transformation leadership roles would be unique. In any case, successful digital transformation will require multiple digital-savvy champions to work as a team for changing the organisation as a whole. So, challenge yourself as a leader for the digital age with regard to each of the leadership types. Combine your strengths with the strengths of others. In the end, it's the team – not the individual – that makes the difference.

THE PARADOX
INVOLVED IN
SCALING AGILITY IS
INTRODUCING
FAST FLEXIBILITY
AND STABILITY
AT THE SAME TIME

CREATING AGILITY
AT SCALE

Organisations must respond and adapt more quickly than ever before. Digital transformation provides opportunities by optimising resource usage, innovating capabilities and creating lasting relationships with customers. Throughout an organisation's journey of digital transformation, agility is one of the most important aspects to be looked at. In this interview, that was first published in the July-August 2019 issue of The European Business Review, Vlerick Business School's professor Stijn Viaene talks about the importance of agile transformation and how it drives and delivers digital transformation.

Question: Scaling agility is a huge topic right now, especially to organisations during their digital transformation journey. Could you tell us exactly what this is about? Does it matter to all organisations?

Stijn Viaene: Agility is what is required from organisations that want to thrive in turbulent environments, like the digital economy. It implies speed, flexibility, and most of all, responsiveness to change.

Today, people almost automatically associate agility with the introduction of self-organising, multidisciplinary teams. These teams are empowered to decide autonomously, without having to escalate decision making all the time. Publicly available models for implementing agile teamwork, such as Scrum[1] or Kanban[2], have become increasingly popular.

Now, if you only have one such a team, which is not too big, composed of highly competent people, and a team with a great team dynamic, then these agile setups can really work miracles. It is what fuels the success of digital startups.

On the other hand, what if you have ten, twenty, eighty or more of these agile teams all running initiatives at the same time? With all sorts of dependencies amongst the teams and the projects, some teams may need the work of others as inputs. Projects of different teams may work with a common data resource. Teams may fight for the same scarce resources and talent. And, what if there's a great deal of legacy around, which the teams need to somehow work with?

This situation easily ends up in chaos, especially when the change has to come fast or very fast as in the digital age.

You will have to find ways to align the different team and project objectives, coordinate resource allocation, and manage to integrate the results without jeopardising the agility of the teams, and that is quite a challenge. This challenge is referred to as scaling agility or creating agility at scale.

Question: You have mentioned the need for aligning, coordinating and integrating work as critical to making agility at scale work. These things are essential in achieving the goals and focus of organisations. Over the years, what changes did you notice in terms of the goals and objectives of different organisations?

Stijn Viaene: The importance of aligning, coordinating and integrating work is not new. It goes back to the very essence of making organisations work.

What has changed though, is the backdrop against which we are organising: turbulence, catalysed by digitalisation.

At the risk of oversimplifying things, you could say that in the past, we organised for focus, cost, efficiency and stability. Today, we are still aiming for focus, but with emphasis on creating speed (i.e. speed-to-market), flexibility and choice.

It does not mean that the former set of objectives is less important in turbulent times, quite the opposite, I would say, but the challenge has shifted very much towards combining these former objectives with the latter ones.

This immediately brings us to the paradox involved in scaling agility: introducing fast flexibility as well as stability at the same time. That is what makes it so hard to get it right. We'll have to effectively figure out where stability matters and where it can be relaxed.

However, one thing is clear: With the speed at which things are moving today, we are no longer able to achieve the right balance between flexibility and stability by relying on our human abilities alone. We'll have to work creatively with digital technologies to help us find and install the right balance between stability and flexibility.

Question: As you have said, stability and flexibility are two major components that should be achieved through scaling agility. How will leaders be able to apply the concept of scaled agility in their respective organisations?

Stijn Viaene: There are several practice frameworks available for scaling agility to the enterprise level. They are all relatively new.

For example, there's SAFe[3] which stands for "Scaled Agile Framework", but there's also LeSS[4] – for "Large Scale Scrum", DAD[5] which is "Disciplined Agile Delivery" and more. Each of these frameworks has its own origins and scope.

One alternative, which many people may have heard of is the "Spotify model",[6] named after the way digital music streaming service Spotify organises for agility at scale. A few years ago, the model got a serious boost when ING banking Group announced that it would emulate it to accelerate its digital transformation. Spotify's model is a nice example for showcasing an organisation that is looking for what I would call a "minimum viable work and organising model".

In Spotify's model, the whole organisation is reconceived into relatively small autonomous, multidisciplinary teams – or "squads". A team has a "product owner", who represents the customer and who helps the team prioritise work. Each squad has end-to-end responsibility for a particular customer value mission.

Squads with closely related missions are grouped into "tribes"; groupings that are not too big, in order not to jeopardise agility. A "tribe lead" – a squad member himself – is responsible for connecting the dots between the squads.

People in the squads are also networked across squads and tribes based on their expertise or discipline. These networks are called "chapters". Chapters are groupings that create economies of scale.

Arguably, chapters are light-weight, light-touch functions. Light-weight, because their experts are supposed to operate from within the squads. There's no big central function team somewhere high-up into the organisation. Light-touch, because the discipline that the experts install for achieving economies of scale should not come at the expense of the squads' ability to deliver customer value fast and frequently. In practice, that's a hard balance to strike.

Finally, Spotify also talks about "guilds". These are, essentially, communities of interest or practice.[7] They work more organically than chapters. They allow people who share a common passion, interest or practice to come together to share experiences, cases and challenges, and even create shared best practices. Guilds promote learning with a bottom-up drive.

Question: With all the diversity of frameworks and methods for scaling agility, in your view, what is the most effective way or mechanism that organisations should implement to become more agile at scale?

Stijn Viaene: What all the frameworks for scaling agility have in common is that they are suggestions. They are works in progress.

Now, for a work in progress to effectively progress, you need constructs in your organised model that stimulate learning, particularly learning by doing. You need mechanisms that allow you to iterate back and forth between acting and thinking to find new and better ways of working.

Personally, I believe that working with communities of practice – or guilds – can be a great mechanism to help organisations effectively learn how to become more agile at scale.

It goes something like this: People start by looking at their agile practices and routines as real-life experiments, they regularly come together to share their experiences and discuss challenges related to their experiments, they then together evaluate which practices work and which don't. They decide to replicate what works and stop and take note of what doesn't work.

This cycle gets repeated at a steady rhythm; a rhythm at which the organisation is able to absorb the proposed changes. The idea is that you get better at this routine over time, allowing you to increase the learning rhythm. This way, the rate of change inside the organisation can be gradually synchronised with the rate of change on the outside.

Working with communities of practice also helps to make your agile and digital transformation inclusive, rather than exclusive. It allows you to shape the transformation as an open invitation for everyone to contribute. This way, the organisation can collectively learn how to do things differently and better, with a view to winning together.

I would be happy to call the people who effectively take up the glove to help drive this collaborative learning journey, leaders. Not the kind of leadership that you'd find in the "How I changed my company" type of stories featuring superstar chief executive officers, but a much more humble, "servant"[8] interpretation of leadership.

In fact, the 4-V model of digital transformation leadership is an invitation to form your own communities of agile leadership practice around the V-roles in the model: Vigilant, Voyager, Visionary, Vested. Working with the model in your organisation offers people an opportunity to take part in learning how to become an agile organisation that routinely explores and exploits digital opportunities faster than its rivals.

Question: As you have mentioned, scaling agility is one of the hardest phases in organisation transformation. What are the common difficulties that organisations could face in their journey to transformation and what advice could you give to leaders for them to succeed in their digital transformation?

Stijn Viaene: It will be crucial to get the whole organisation to work together in the same agile ways. That means introducing agility at the level of individuals, teams and the organisation, as a whole. Only then will your digital transformation succeed. And that's exactly what working with the 4-V model aspires.

All too often, unfortunately, the introduction of the notion of agility and its implementation at the different organisational levels are done in a very unorderly fashion. There is no common frame, no common language, different support teams, little governance, etc.

That's a proven recipe for disaster. Leadership has a vested interest not to let this happen.

My advice is this:

- Introduce customer-centricity as the number one unifying principle for your transformation.
- Organise around customer value missions. Make small multidisciplinary teams, working iteratively and with fast customer feedback, responsible and accountable for creating and delivering customer value within the missions.
- Learn how to make agile teamwork successful. Also, and most importantly, invest in learning how to align, coordinate and integrate these agile teams into an agile organisation that is more than the sum of its agile teams. Create communities of agile leadership practice along the lines of the 4-V model to accelerate these learning processes.
- Invest in the power of digital technologies to create future-proof agility at scale.

THE ONLY PREREQUISITES TO LEADERSHIP ARE THAT YOU REMAIN POSITIVE, CALM AND OPEN-MINDED

Alexis Hunter

ABOUT THE AUTHOR

Stijn Viaene is a professor and partner at Vlerick Business School, where he serves as the Director of the focus area Digital Transformation. He is also a professor at the Research Center for Information System Engineering (LIRIS) at KU Leuven. Previously, he was the Deloitte Chair Professor of Bringing IT to Board Level at Vlerick Business School. At KU Leuven, he was holder of the VDAB Research Chair of Digital Innovation in Public Services and the Amsterdam-Amstelland Research Chair for Intelligence-Led Policing. He received a PhD from KU Leuven for his work on using machine learning to detect fraud from enriched insurance claims data.

Stijn loves solving managerial puzzles around investments in digital technologies. His teaching, research and counselling focus on four primary areas: digital innovation and transformation, business and IT alignment, business analytics, and business process management. He is involved in various research initiatives in collaboration with industry and public sector partners. His research has been published in outlets such as MIT Sloan Management Review, Communications of the ACM, The European Business Review, Ivey Business Journal, Information and Management, IEEE IT Professional, Government Information Quarterly, Technological Forecasting & Social Change, Expert Systems with Applications, Machine Learning. Stijn is a passionate teacher. He loves working with teaching cases and has written several himself.

ENDNOTES

1   Quotation from Alan Kay, in Munro, A. (1984). "Alan Kay Thinks the Computer You Just Bought Is 'No Big Deal'." ST.Mac. April. https://yesterbits.com/media/pubs/STMac/st.mac-1984-apr-300dpi.pdf.

Digital transformation, so what?

1   Brynjolfsson, E. and McAfee, A. (2014). *The Second Machine Age: Work, Progress, and Prosperity in a Time of Brilliant Technologies*. New York (NY): W.W. Norton & Company.

2   Ante, S.E. (2011). "Computer Conquers 'Jeopardy!'." The Wall Street Journal. January 14. https://www.wsj.com/articles/SB10001424052748704307404576080333201294262.

3   Grossman, L. (2011). "2045: The Year Man Becomes Immortal." Time Magazine. February 10. http://content.time.com/time/magazine/article/0,9171,2048299,00.html.

4   Kurzweil, R. (2006). *The Singularity Is Near: When Humans Transcend Biology*. New York (NY): Penguin Books.

5   Ibid., jacket quote by Bill Gates. http://www.singularity.com/aboutthebook.html, accessed November 25, 2019.

6   Kurzweil, R. (2010). "10 Questions to Ray Kurzweil." Time Magazine. December 10. http://content.time.com/time/magazine/article/0,9171,2033076,00.html.

7   Innovation is defined as "the market introduction of a technical or organisational novelty, not just its invention", in Schumpeter, J.A. (1934 [1983]). *The Theory of Economic Development: An Inquiry into Profits, Capital, Credit, Interest and the Business Cycle (Introduction by J.E. Elliott)*. Translated from German by R. Opie. London (UK): Transaction Publishers. Schumpeter emphasises the difference between invention and innovation,

143

because "as long as they are not carried into practice, inventions are economically irrelevant".

8   According to https://en.wikipedia.com, fintech, a portmanteau of "financial technology" is used to describe "the technology and innovation that aims to compete with traditional financial methods in the delivery of financial services. It is an emerging industry that uses technology to improve activities in finance." https://en.wikipedia.org/wiki/Financial_technology, accessed November 25, 2019.

9   A business model describes how a business creates and captures value. It is composed of three interconnected elements: (1) value for the customer (i.e. customer value proposition), (2) value for the business (i.e. business profit formula), (3) key resources and processes necessary to deliver value for the customer and value for the business. For more on business models, see Magretta, J. et al. (2019). *On Business Model Innovation*. HBR's 10 Must Reads. Boston (MA): Harvard Business Review Press.

10   See, for example, Christensen, C.M. (1997). *The Innovator's Dilemma: When New Technologies Cause Great Firms to Fail*. Boston (MA): Harvard Business School Press; and Christensen, C.M. and Raynor, M.E. (2013). *The Innovator's Solution: Creating and Sustaining Successful Growth*. Boston (MA): Harvard Business Review Press.

11   Downes, L. and Nunes, P. (2014). *Big Bang Disruption: Strategy in the Age of Devastating Innovation*. New York (NY): Portfolio Penguin.

12   For more on the combinatorial nature of digital innovation, see Brynjolfsson and McAfee, *The Second Machine Age*.

13   Kanter, R.M. (2012). "The Business Ecosystem." Harvard Magazine. September-October. https://harvardmagazine.com/2012/09/the-business-ecosystem.

14   Viaene, S. (2017). "A Digital Quick-Start Guide." Ivey Business Journal. September-October. https://iveybusinessjournal.com/a-digital-quick-start-guide.

Rethinking strategy for the digital age

The first version of this chapter was published as Viaene, S. (2017). "Rethinking Strategy for the Digital Age: An Executive Primer." The European Business Review. July-August.

1   For example, every year Gartner creates more than hundred "hype cycles" in various technology domains to track maturity and potential. For more on Gartner's hype cycles, see Fenn, J. and Blosch, M. (2018). "Understanding

Gartner's Hype Cycles." Gartner ID: G00370163. https://www.gartner.com/en/documents/3887767/understanding-gartner-s-hype-cycles.

2   Quotation from Drucker, P.F. (1980). *Managing in Turbulent Times*. New York (NY): Harper and Row.

3   "An organisation's core capabilities are those activities that, when performed at the highest level, enable the organisation to bring its where-to-play and how-to-win choices to life", according to Lafley, A.G. and Martin, R. L. (2013). *Playing to Win: How Strategy Really Works*. Boston (MA): Harvard Business Review Press. For more on organisational capabilities, see Amit, R. and Schoemaker, P.J.H. (1993). "Strategic Assets and Organizational Rent." Strategic Management Journal. 14(1). According to Amit and Schoemaker organisational capabilities refer to "a firm's capacity to deploy resources, usually in combination, using organizational processes, to effect a desired end. They are information-based, tangible or intangible processes that are firm specific and are developed over time through complex interactions among the firm's resources. They can abstractly be thought of as 'intermediate goods' generated by the firm to provide enhanced productivity of its resources, as well as strategic flexibility and protection for its final product or service. Unlike resources, capabilities are based on developing, carrying, and exchanging information through the firm's human capital." Amit and Schoemaker define an organisation's core capabilities as "strategic assets", that is, "the set of difficult to trade and imitate, scarce, appropriable and specialized resources and capabilities that bestow the firm's competitive advantage".

4   Lafley and Martin, *Playing to Win*.

5   For more on using scenarios for strategic planning, see Ramirez, R. and Wilkinson, A. (2016). *Strategic Reframing: The Oxford Scenario Planning Approach*. Oxford (UK): Oxford University Press; and Schoemaker, P.J.H. (1995). "Scenario Planning: A Tool for Strategic Thinking." MIT Sloan Management Review. 36(2). https://sloanreview.mit.edu/article/scenario-planning-a-tool-for-strategic-thinking.

6   See Verweire, K., Viaene, S. and De Prins, P. (2017). KBC's Digital Transformation: A Strategic Response. In A. Janes and C. Sutton (Eds.). *Crafting and Executing Strategy*. 2nd International Edition. London (UK): McGraw-Hill Education.

7   During an investor visit to Ireland in June 2017, KBC Group's chief executive officer Johan Thijs announced that KBC intended to invest a further 1.5 billion euros in digital transformation between 2017 and year-end 2020; see KBC Group (2017). "Today's KBC Investor Visit to Ireland." June 21. https://www.kbc.com/en/system/files/doc/newsroom/pressreleases/2017/20170621_Onsitevisit_Ireland_en.pdf.

8   Verweire, Viaene and De Prins, KBC's Digital Transformation.

9   Ibid.

10   Johan Thijs, interview with Stijn Viaene, June 30, 2016.

11   There are many variations of this growth portfolio model. One of the most popular ones is McKinsey's Three Horizons of Growth, in Baghai, M., Coley, S. and White, D. (1999). *The Alchemy of Growth: Practical Insights for Building the Enduring Enterprise*. London (UK): Orion Business; also note Steve Blank's 2019 article, "McKinsey's Three Horizons Model Defined Innovation for Years. Here's Why It No Longer Applies." Harvard Business Review. February 1. https://hbr.org/2019/02/mckinseys-three-horizons-model-defined-innovation-for-years-heres-why-it-no-longer-applies. Blank's main thesis is that the model's time-based definition made sense in the 20th century when new disruptive ideas took years to research, engineer and deliver. That, he argues, is no longer true in the 21st century.

12   See Viaene, S. (2019). "KPN: How to Navigate the Digital Tides." Ivey ID: 9B19M046. London (Canada): Ivey Publishing.

13   According to https://en.wikipedia.com, net promoter score (NPS) is "a management tool that can be used to gauge the loyalty of a firm's customer relationships. It serves as an alternative to traditional customer satisfaction research and is claimed to be correlated with revenue growth. NPS has been widely adopted with more than two thirds of Fortune 1,000 companies using the metric. The tool aims to measure the loyalty that exists between a provider and a consumer." https://en.wikipedia.org/wiki/Net_Promoter, accessed November 27, 2019.

14   Viaene, "KPN: How to Navigate the Digital Tides."

15   See https://www.tmforum.org/business-process-framework, accessed November 25, 2019.

16   See Viaene, S. (2018). "UCB: Data is the New Drug." Ivey ID: 9B18E002. London (Canada): Ivey Publishing.

17   Viaene, "KPN: How to Navigate the Digital Tides."

18   Day, G.S. (2007). "Is It Real? Can We Win? Is It Worth Doing? Managing Risk and Reward in an Innovation Portfolio." Harvard Business Review. December. https://hbr.org/2007/12/is-it-real-can-we-win-is-it-worth-doing-managing-risk-and-reward-in-an-innovation-portfolio.

19   See Gilbert, C., Eyring, M. and Foster, R.N. (2012). "Two Routes to Resilience." Harvard Business Review. December. https://hbr.org/2012/12/two-routes-to-resilience.

20   Govindarajan, V. and Trimble, C. (2005). "Organizational DNA for Strategic Innovation." California Management Review. 47(3).

21   Ibid.

22   Govindarajan, V. and Trimble, C. (2005). *Ten Rules for Strategic Innovators: From Idea to Execution*. Boston (MA): Harvard Business School Press.

23   Viaene, "KPN: How to Navigate the Digital Tides."

Digital reality no. 1: Customer experience is value

The first version of this chapter was published as Viaene, S. (2017). "Digital Reality No.1: Customer Experience is Value." The European Business Review. September-October.

1   See https://www.motif.com/motifs/couch-commerce, accessed November 27, 2019.

2   See https://www.motif.com/motifs/rest-in-peace, accessed November 27, 2019.

3   Quotation from Benjamin Franklin, in https://en.wikipedia.org/wiki/Death_and_taxes_(idiom), accessed November 25, 2019.

4   According to https://en.wikipedia.com, robo-advisors are "a class of financial advisor that provide financial advice or investment management online with moderate to minimal human intervention. They provide digital financial advice based on mathematical rules or algorithms." https://en.wikipedia.org/wiki/Robo-advisor, accessed November 27, 2019.

5   Tagline from Motif Investing, in AWI Ventures, KPMG Australia, Financial Services Council (2014). "The 50 Best Fintech Innovators Report 2014." December. https://www.planet-fintech.com/file/163911.

6   Pine, J. and Gilmore, J. (1999). *The Experience Economy*. Boston (MA): Harvard Business School Press.

7   Christensen, C.M. and Raynor, M.E. (2013). *The Innovator's Solution: Creating and Sustaining Successful Growth*. Boston (MA): Harvard Business Review Press.

8   Christensen, C.M., Hall, T., Dillon, K. and Duncan, D.S. (2016). "Know Your Customers' 'Jobs to Be Done'." Harvard Business Review. September. https://hbr.org/2016/09/know-your-customers-jobs-to-be-done.

9   Brown, T. (2008). "Design Thinking." Harvard Business Review. June. https://hbr.org/2008/06/design-thinking. For more on design thinking, see Brown, T. and Katz, B. (2019). *Change by Design, Revised and Updated: How Design Thinking Transforms Organizations and Inspires Innovation*. New York (NY): Harper Business; and Knapp, J., Zeratsky, J. and Kowitz, B. (2016). *Sprint: How to Solve Big Problems and Test New Ideas in Just Five Days*. New York (NY): Simon & Schuster; see also The Hasso Plattner Institute of Design (d.school) at Stanford University, https://dschool.stanford.edu, accessed November 28, 2019.

10   For more on "agile's emergence as a huge global movement extending beyond software", see Denning, S. (2018). "What is Agile?" Forbes. August 13. https://www.forbes.com/sites/stevedenning/2016/08/13/what-is-agile/#3256040126e3.

11   For more on customer (experience) journey mapping, see Følstad, A. and Kvale, K. (2018). "Customer Journeys: A Systematic Literature Review." Journal of Service Theory and Practice. 28(2); Kalbach, J. (2016). *Mapping Experiences: A Complete Guide to Creating Value through Journeys, Blueprints and Diagrams*. Sebastopol (CA): O'Reilly Media; and HM Government (2007). "Customer Journey Mapping: Guide for Practitioners." https://www.behaviourchange.net/download/232-customer-journey-mapping-guide-for-practitioners.

12   Customer journey map template based on the discussion in HM Government, "Customer Journey Mapping: Guide for Practitioners."

13   Osterwalder, A. and Pigneur, Y. (2010). *Business Model Generation: A Handbook for Visionaries, Game Changers and Challengers*. Hoboken (NJ): John Wiley and Sons.

14   This picture of Osterwalder and Pigneur's business model canvas was redrawn and adapted, to indicate desirability, feasibility and viability articulation, from the original, in https://www.strategyzer.com/canvas, accessed November 25, 2019.

15   See, for example, Stanford d.school (2010). "An Introduction to Design Thinking Process Guide." https://dschool-old.stanford.edu/sandbox/groups/designresources/wiki/36873/attachments/74b3d/ModeGuideBOOTCAMP2010L.pdf.

16   This picture of Stanford d.school's design thinking process was redrawn and adapted from the original on the 88tc88 Blog, as referenced in Zaman, K. (2013). "Calm Before the Brainstorm – Design Thinking for Agencies." February 23. https://kashifzaman.com/design-thinking/.

17   Maurya, A. (2016). *Scaling Lean: Mastering the Key Metrics for Startup Growth*. New York (NY): Portfolio Penguin.

18   From https://www.designabetterbusiness.tools/tools/experiment-canvas, accessed November 25, 2019.

19   According to MIT's Center for Information Systems Research (CISR), "from a technical perspective, a blockchain is a trail of transaction blocks that have been linked to together in an immutable way. More generally, blockchain is a label for the subset of distributed ledger technologies that create the chain and transact on it, including distributed ledgers, consensus protocols, and tokens/digital assets." https://cisr.mit.edu/research/research-overview/blockchain/blockchain-glossary, accessed November 25, 2019. For more on blockchain, see Tapscott, D. et al. (2018). *Preparing for a Blockchain*

Future. MIT Sloan Management Review. Special Collection. November 22; and Furlonger, D. and Uzureau, C. (2019). *The Real Business of Blockchain: How Leaders Can Create Value in a New Digital Age.* Boston (MA): Harvard Business Review Press.

20   Beck, K. et al. (2001). "Manifesto for Agile Software Development (Agile Manifesto)." February. https://agilemanifesto.org, accessed November 25, 2019.

21   For an adapted version of the Agile Manifesto's four values, extending them to agile methodologies beyond software engineering, see Rigby, D.K., Sutherland, J. and Takeuchi, J. (2016). "Embracing Agile." Harvard Business Review. May.

22   Scrum creators Ken Schwaber and Jeff Sutherland defined Scrum as "a framework within which people can address complex adaptive problems, while productively and creatively delivering products of the highest possible value", in Schwaber, K. and Sutherland, J. (2017). "The Scrum Guide, The Definitive Guide to Scrum: The Rules of the Game." November. https://scrumguides.org/scrum-guide.html, accessed November 27, 2019.

23   See https://www.gartner.com/en/information-technology/glossary/devops, accessed November 26, 2019.

24   For more on devops, see High, P. (2015). "An Introduction to DevOps From One of Its Godfathers." Forbes. February 23. https://www.forbes.com/sites/peterhigh/2015/02/23/an-introduction-to-devops-from-its-godfather/#5ee3b658b785; Kim, G. and Willis, J. (2018). *Beyond the Phoenix Project: The Origins and Evolution of DevOps.* Portland (OR): IT Revolution Press; and Leite, L., Rocha, C., Kon, F., Milojicic, D. and Meirelles, P. (2019). "A Survey of DevOps Concepts and Challenges." ACM Computing Surveys. 52(6).

25   Gnanasambandam, C., Harrysson, M., Mangla, R. and Srivastava, S. (2017). "An Executive Guide to Software Development." McKinsey Insights. February. https://www.mckinsey.com/business-functions/mckinsey-digital/our-insights/an-executives-guide-to-software-development.

26   Ries, E. (2011). *The Lean Startup: How Today's Entrepreneurs Use Continuous Innovation to Create Radically Successful Businesses.* New York (NY): Crown Business.

27   For more on customer-validated learning, see Ries, E. (2009). "Validated Learning About Customers." April 14. https://www.startuplessonslearned.com/2009/04/validated-learning-about-customers.html.

28   For more on build-measure-learn, see Ries, E. (2010). "Good Enough Never Is (Or Is It?)." September 27. https://www.startuplessonslearned.com/2010/09/good-enough-never-is-or-is-it.html.

29   Ries, E. (2009). "Lessons Learned: Minimum Viable Product: A Guide." August 3. https://www.startuplessonslearned.com/2009/08/minimum-viable-product-guide.html.

30 For more on business process management (BPM), see vom Brocke, J., Schmiedel, T., Recker, J., Trkman, P., Mertens, W. and Viaene, S. (2014). "Ten Principles of Good Business Process Management." Business Process Management Journal. 20(4); and Hammer, M. (2015). What is Business Process Management? In J. vom Brocke and M. Rosemann (Eds.). *Handbook of Business Process Management 1*. International Handbooks on Information Systems. 2nd Edition. Berlin Heidelberg (Germany): Springer-Verlag.

31 Lyons, D. (2009). "'We Start with the Customer and We Work Backward', Jeff Bezos on Amazon's Success." Slate.com. December 24. https://slate.com/news-and-politics/2009/12/jeff-bezos-on-amazon-s-success.html.

32 For more on Amazon's obsessing over customers, see Bezos, J.P. (2016). 2015 Letter to Shareholders. In *2016 Annual Report Amazon.com*. January. https://ir.aboutamazon.com/static-files/f124548c-5d0b-41a6-a670-d85bb191fcec.

33 Onetto, M. (2014). "When Toyota Met E-commerce: Lean at Amazon." McKinsey Quarterly. February. https://www.mckinsey.com/business-functions/operations/our-insights/when-toyota-met-e-commerce-lean-at-amazon.

How to catch a moving target

The first version of this chapter was published as Viaene, S. (2017). "How to Catch a Moving Target in the Digital World." The European Business Review. November-December.

1 Davenport, T.H. and Harris, J.G. (2017). *Competing on Analytics: Updated with a New Introduction: The New Science of Winning*. Boston (MA): Harvard Business Review Press.

2 In 1999, Philip Evans and Thomas Wurster described the transfer of information as a trade-off between richness and reach, and predicted that with the arrival of e-commerce the trade-off would be broken; see Evans, P. and Wurster, T.S. (1999). *Blown to Bits: How the New Economics of Information Transforms Strategy*. Boston (MA): Harvard Business Review Press.

3 ING Group (2015). "2014 Annual Report ING Group." March. https://www.ing.com/About-us/Annual-reporting-suite/Annual-Reports-archive.htm, accessed November 26, 2019.

4 Ibid.

5 Ibid.

6 ING Group (2016). "ING Strategy Update: Accelerating Think Forward." October 3. Amsterdam (the Netherlands). https://www.ing.com/Newsroom/News/Press-releases/ING-strategy-update-Accelerating-Think-Forward.htm.

7 Ibid.

8   Ibid.

9   ING Group (2017). "2016 Annual Report ING Group." March. https://www.ing.com/About-us/Annual-reporting-suite/Annual-Reports-archive.htm, accessed November 26, 2019.

10   For more on the growing importance of business analytics, see, for example, Henke, N., Bughin, J., Chui, M., Manyika, J., Saleh, T., Wiseman, B. and Sethupathy, G. (2016). "The Age of Analytics: Competing in a Data-Driven World." McKinsey Insights. December. https://www.mckinsey.com/business-functions/mckinsey-analytics/our-insights/the-age-of-analytics-competing-in-a-data-driven-world; Ransbotham, S. and Kiron, D. (2017). "Analytics as a Source of Business Innovation." MIT Sloan Management Review. February 28. https://sloanreview.mit.edu/projects/analytics-as-a-source-of-business-innovation; and Ransbotham, S. and Kiron, D. (2018). "Using Analytics to Improve Customer Engagement." MIT Sloan Management Review. January 30. https://sloanreview.mit.edu/projects/using-analytics-to-improve-customer-engagement.

11   Kart, L., Linden, A. and Schulte, W.R. (2013). "Extend Your Portfolio of Analytics Capabilities." Gartner ID: G00254653. September 23.

12   Davenport and Harris, *Competing on Analytics*.

13   This latency categorisation was adapted from the original BI latency discussion, in Hackathorn, R. (2004). "The BI Watch: Real-Time to Real-Value." DM Review. 14(1).

14   The picture of the four types of analytics questions was redrawn and adapted from the original, in Kart, Linden and Schulte, "Extend Your Portfolio of Analytics Capabilities." The latency categories at the bottom of the picture were added, based on an adaption of the original BI latency discussion, in Hackathorn, "The BI Watch: Real-Time to Real-Value."

15   See, for example, Stylianou, N., Nurse, T., Fletcher, G., Fewster, A., Bangay, R. and Walton, J. (2015). "Will a Robot Take Your Job?" BBC News – Technology. September 11. https://www.bbc.com/news/technology-34066941, accessed November 26, 2019.

16   Estimates by Tabb Group (https://www.tabbgroup.com), in World Federation of Exchanges (2013). "Understanding High Frequency Trading." May 29.

17   Davenport and Harris, *Competing on Analytics*.

18   Enedis (2017). "Key Figures 2017." https://www.enedis.fr/sites/default/files/2017_key_figures.PDF.

19   See Viaene, S., Momber, I. and Meeus, L. (2017). "Enedis: Market Maker, Not Market Taker." Case Centre ID: 317-0001-1. January.

20   Ibid.

21   Ibid.

22 Ibid.

23 Hopkins, M.S. (2010). "The Four Ways IT is Revolutionizing Innovation (Interview with Erik Brynjolfsson)." MIT Sloan Management Review. 51(3). https://sloanreview.mit.edu/article/it-innovation-brynjolfsson-article.

24 Ibid.

25 Davenport, T.H. and Patil, D.J. (2012). "Data Scientist: The Sexiest Job of the 21st Century." Harvard Business Review, October. https://hbr.org/2012/10/data-scientist-the-sexiest-job-of-the-21st-century.

26 Boucher Fergusson, R. (2012). "It's All About the Platform: What Walmart and Google Have in Common." MIT Sloan Management Review. December 5. https://sloanreview.mit.edu/article/its-all-about-the-platform-what-walmart-and-google-have-in-common.

27 Viaene, S. (2013). "Data Scientists Aren't Domain Experts." IEEE IT Professional. 15(6).

28 This picture was redrawn and adapted from the original, in Viaene, "Data Scientists Aren't Domain Experts."

29 Boucher Fergusson, "It's All About the Platform."

30 Based on Viaene, S. (2011). "The Secrets to Managing Business Analytics Projects." MIT Sloan Management Review. 53(1); and Viaene, "Data Scientists Aren't Domain Experts."

31 See, for example, Erwin, T. et al. (2018). "Guardians of Trust: Who Is Responsible for Trusted Analytics in the Digital Age?" KPMG International. February. https://home.kpmg/content/dam/kpmg/xx/pdf/2018/02/guardians-of-trust.pdf.

Digital partnership strategies revealed

The first version of this chapter was published as Viaene, S. (2019). "Digital Partnership Strategies Revealed." The European Business Review. March-April.

1 Atluri, V., Dietz, M. and Henke, N. (2017). "Competing in a World of Sectors Without Borders." McKinsey Quarterly. July. https://www.mckinsey.com/business-functions/mckinsey-analytics/our-insights/competing-in-a-world-of-sectors-without-borders.

2 Iansiti, M. and Levien, R. (2004). "Strategy as Ecology." Harvard Business Review. March. https://hbr.org/2004/03/strategy-as-ecology; see also Iansiti, M. and Levien, R. (2004). *The Keystone Advantage: What the New Dynamics of Business Ecosystems Mean for Strategy, Innovation, and Sustainability*. Boston (MA): Harvard Business School Publishing.

3   See Moore, J.F. (1993). "Predators and Prey: A New Ecology of
      Competition." Harvard Business Review. 71(3); and Moore, J.F. (1996). *The
      Death of Competition: Leadership and Strategy in the Age of Business Ecosystems*.
      New York (NY): Harper Business.

4   For more on companies holding leadership roles in business ecosystems, see
      Iansiti and Levien, *The Keystone Advantage*.

5   Moore, *The Death of Competition*.

6   Adner, R. (2012). *The Wide Lens: A New Strategy for Innovation*. New York
      (NY): Portfolio Penguin.

7   Ibid.

8   The process described in this chapter adheres to a broader class of mapping
      analysis called "value network analysis" (VNA). For more, see Allee, V.
      and Schwabe, O. (2015). *Value Networks and the True Nature of Collaboration*.
      Tampa (FL): Meghan-Kiffer Press; and den Ouden, E. (2012). *Innovation
      Design: Creating Value for People, Organizations and Society*. London (UK):
      Springer-Verlag.

9   This classification of value exchanges was proposed by den Ouden in
      Innovation Design.

10   Porter, M.E. and Heppelmann, J.E. (2014). "How Smart, Connected
      Products Are Changing Competition." Harvard Business Review.
      November. https://hbr.org/2014/11/how-smart-connected-products-are-
      transforming-competition.

11   A useful tool for mapping value paths in more detail is the "value blueprint"
      by Adner, in *The Wide Lens*.

12   See https://en.wikipedia.org/wiki/Acquisition_of_21st_Century_Fox_by_
      Disney, accessed November 27, 2019.

13   For more on collaborative innovation between startups and corporates,
      see Altendorf, M. et al. (2018). "Collaboration Between Start-ups and
      Corporates: A Practical Guide for Mutual Understanding." World Economic
      Forum. January. http://www3.weforum.org/docs/WEF_White_Paper_
      Collaboration_between_Start-ups_and_Corporates.pdf.

14   See https://developer.capitalone.com.

15   See https://developer.capitalone.com/products, accessed November 27, 2019.

16   See https://www.techstars.com/startup-week, accessed November 27, 2019.

17   See https://www.techstars.com/startup-digest, accessed November 27, 2019.

18   See https://www.techstars.com/startup-accelerator, accessed November 27,
      2019.

19   See https://www.techstars.com/programs/arcadis-program, accessed
      November 27, 2019.

20 See https://www.techstars.com/programs/music-program, accessed November 27, 2019.

21 Karpis, P. (2017). "Want to Get into a Top Startup Accelerator? Try These 3 Strategies." Forbes. May 30. https://www.forbes.com/sites/paulinaguditch/2017/05/30/get-into-a-top-startup-accelerator/#5e1fedb1725f.

22 See https://www.techstars.com/companies/#top-50, accessed November 19, 2019.

What digital leadership does

The first version of this chapter was published as Viaene, S. (2017). "What Digital Leadership Does." The European Business Review. May-June. This chapter also incorporates results originally published as Viaene (2018). "Orchestrating Organisational Agility." Ivey Business Journal. March-April.

1 Quotation from Welch, J.F.Jr., Immelt, J.R., Dammerman, D.D. and Wright, R.C. (2001). To Our Customers, Share Owners and Employees. In *2000 Annual Report GE*. February. https://www.ge.com/annual00/download/images/GEannual00.pdf.

2 Organisational practices are defined as "embodied, materially mediated arrays of human activity centrally organized around shared practical understanding", in Schatzki, T.R. (2001). Introduction: Practice Theory. In T.R. Schatzki, K. Knorr Cetina and E. von Savigny. (Eds.). *The Practice Turn in Contemporary Theory*. New York (NY): Routledge. For more on the "practice turn" in organising theory that is aimed at shedding a more comprehensive light on modern-day issues of organising and work, see Smets, M., Aristidou, A. and Whittington, R. (2017). Towards a Practice-Driven Institutionalism. In R. Greenwood, C. Oliver, T.B. Lawrence and R. Meyer (Eds.). *The Sage Handbook of Organizational Institutionalism*. 2nd Edition. London (UK): Sage.

3 Miroslaw Forystek, interview with Stijn Viaene, January 24, 2017.

4 For inspiration on vigilance tools and practices, see, for example, Day, G.S. and Schoemaker, P.J.H. (2019). *See Sooner, Act Faster: How Vigilant Leaders Thrive in an Era of Digital Turbulence*. Boston (MA): The MIT Press.

5 See Veugelers, M., Bury, J. and Viaene, S. (2010). "Linking Technology Intelligence to Open Innovation." Technological Forecasting and Social Change. 77(2).

6 Ibid.

7 Mark Veugelers, interview with Stijn Viaene, March 24, 2017.

8   Garry Lyons, interview with Stijn Viaene, February 23, 2015.

9   See, for example, Mastercard (2010). "Mastercard Launches Mastercard
    Labs; Names Garry Lyons Group Executive, Research & Development."
    April 15. https://newsroom.mastercard.com/press-releases/mastercard-
    launches-mastercard-labs-names-garry-lyons-group-executive-research-
    development/; Fast Company (2014). "Inside Mastercard's Innovation
    Labs." May 12. https://www.fastcompany.com/3039211/inside-mastercards-
    innovation-labs; and Jackson, B. (2016). "Mastercard Brings 'Labs as
    a Service' to Canadian HQ." IT World Canada. July 26. https://www.
    itworldcanada.com/article/mastercard-brings-labs-as-a-service-to-canadian-
    hq/395128.

10 Ries, *The Lean Startup*.

11 See Viaene, S. and Danneels, L. (2016). "Innovating with Career Analytics
    and Big Data." Case Centre ID: 316-0099-1. February; and Danneels,
    L. and Viaene, S. (2015). "Simple Rules Strategy to Transform Government:
    An ADR Approach." Government Information Quarterly. 32(4).

12 Niels Tanésy, interview with Stijn Viaene, November 15, 2019.

13 See Danneels and Viaene, "Simple Rules Strategy to Transform
    Government."

14 See Benioff, M. and Adler, C. (2009). *Behind the Cloud: The Untold Story of
    How Salesforce.com Went from Idea to Billion-Dollar Company – and Revolutionized
    an Industry*. San Francisco (CA): Jossey-Bass.

15 See Porter and Heppelmann, "How Smart, Connected Products Are
    Changing Competition."

16 See, for example, Bloomberg Surveillance (2015). "Met Tries to Tell
    Stories About Its Art (Interview with Sreenath Sreenivasan)." https://www.
    bloomberg.com/news/videos/2015-04-07/met-tries-to-tell-stories-about-its-
    art-sreenivasan.

17 See Christensen and Raynor, *The Innovator's Solution*.

18 Greater London Authority (2013). "Smart London Plan." December.
    https://www.london.gov.uk/sites/default/files/smart_london_plan.pdf; see
    also Greater London Authority (2016). "The Future of Smart: Harnessing
    Digital Innovation to Make London the Best City in the World. Update
    Report of the Smart London Plan (2013)." March. https://www.london.gov.
    uk/sites/default/files/gla_smartlondon_report_web_4.pdf.

19 See https://data.london.gov.uk.

20 Greater London Authority (2016). "Data for London: A City Data Strategy."
    March. https://files.datapress.com/london/dataset/data-for-london-a-
    city-data-strategy/2016-05-19T15:39:34/London%20City%20Data%20
    Strategy%20March%202016.pdf.

21 See https://www.sidewalktoronto.ca, accessed November 28, 2019; see also Oliver, J. (2019). "Sidewalk Labs Reaches Smart-City Deal with Toronto." Financial Times. October 31.

22 Peter Oosterveer, interview with Stijn Viaene, September 19, 2018.

23 For more on BIM, see "The Benefits of BIM" by Autodesk, https://www. autodesk.com/solutions/bim/benefits-of-bim, accessed November 28, 2019; The British Standards Institution (BSI). "What is BIM?" https://www. bsigroup.com/en-GB/Building-Information-Modelling-BIM/, accessed November 28, 2019; and Naden, C. (2019). "Better Building with New International Standards for BIM." January 21. https://www.iso.org/news/ ref2364.html.

24 In 2018, BSI published a whitepaper, "BIM and Beyond: Digital Transformation in the Built Environment", stating that the construction industry is "moving the production of building information from an individual, non-collaborative, two-dimensional approach (Level 0) to a fully digital environment encouraging full collaboration (BIM Level 3). Currently, however, Level 3 has not yet been fully defined and no organization is yet recognized as working beyond Level 2." https:// www.bsigroup.com/LocalFiles/nl-NL/product-certification/kitemark/ downloads/BSI-BIM-Whitepaper-web-NL-en.pdf. Also, on their website, BSI announced a one-day BIM workshop for February 27, 2020 with the announcement that "attention is now turning to the nature and implications of BIM Level 3 and beyond; including social integration, SmartCities (Communities), Geographical Information Systems (GIS), Internet of Things (IoT) and Smart Contracts. BIM Level 3 is still being defined and developed, but the direction of travel is clear – better linkages between datasets, wider and deeper data about the beneficial use of built environment assets, greater automation of data-handling, and societal outcomes; not just technical outputs." https://www.bsigroup.com/en-GB/our-services/training-courses/BIM-training-courses/bim-digital-built-britain-bim-level-3-iot-and-smartcities/, accessed November 28, 2019.

25 Bram Mommers, picture sent in an email to Stijn Viaene, December 20, 2017.

26 Julien Cayet, interview with Stijn Viaene, April 26, 2018.

27 Arcadis (2019). "Global Digital Strategy." Internal document. June.

28 Ibid.

29 For more on EA, see Cumps, B., Viaene, S., Dussart, P. and Vanden Brande, J. (2013). "Towards Enterprise Architecture Infused Organizations." Journal of Enterprise Architecture. 9(2); Bontinck, G., Cumps, B., Viaene, S., Bille, W. and Vanden Brande, J. (2018). "From Enterprise Architect to Opportunity Architect: The Changing Role of Enterprise Architecture in a Digital Transformation Context." Journal of Enterprise Architecture. 12(4);

and Ross, J.W., Weill, P. and Robertson, D.C. (2006). *Enterprise Architecture as Strategy: Creating a Foundation for Business Execution*. Boston (MA): Harvard Business School Press.

30   Ross, J.W., Beath, C.M. and Sebastian, I. (2015). "Why Nordstrom's Digital Strategy Works (and Yours Probably Doesn't)." Harvard Business Review, January 14. https://hbr.org/2015/01/why-nordstroms-digital-strategy-works-and-yours-probably-doesnt.

31   Ibid.

32   See Viaene, "KPN: How to Navigate the Digital Tides."

33   Ibid.

34   In 2014, Henrik Kniberg, an agile/lean coach working mostly with Lego and Spotify, explained the agile way of working at Spotify in two videos on the Spotify Labs blog. See Kniberg, H. (2014). "Spotify Engineering Culture (Parts 1 and 2)." March 27. https://labs.spotify.com/2014/03/27/spotify-engineering-culture-part-1/, accessed November 28, 2019.

35   See Viaene, "UCB: Data Is the New Drug."

36   Jean-Christophe Tellier, interview with Stijn Viaene, September 2, 2016.

37   Communities of practice are defined as "groups of people who share a concern, a set of problems, or a passion about a topic, and who deepen their knowledge and expertise in this area by interacting on an ongoing basis", in Wenger, E., McDermott, R. and Snyder, W.M. (2002). *A Guide to Managing Knowledge: Cultivating Communities of Practice*. Boston (MA): Harvard Business School Press.

Creating agility at scale

This interview was first published as Viaene, S. (2019). "Scaling Agility: The Fuel that Drives the Organisation's Digital Transformation." The European Business Review. July-August.

1   See Schwaber and Sutherland, "The Scrum Guide."

2   According to https://en.wikipedia.org/, Kanban, from the Japanese, signboard or billboard, "is a lean method to manage and improve work across human systems. This approach aims to manage work by balancing demands with available capacity, and by improving the handling of system-level bottlenecks." https://en.wikipedia.org/wiki/Kanban_(development), accessed November 28, 2019. For more on the combination of Kanban and Scrum for agile software development, see Kniberg, H. and Skarin, M. (2010). *Kanban and Scrum – Making the Most of Both (Enterprise Software Development)*. Toronto (Canada): C4Media.

3   See https://www.scaledagileframework.com, accessed November 29, 2019.

4   See https://less.works, accessed November 29, 2019.

5   See https://disciplinedagiledelivery.com, accessed November 29, 2019.

6   See Kniberg, "Spotify Engineering Culture."

7   See Wenger, McDermott and Snyder, *A Guide to Managing Knowledge*.

8   For more on servant leadership, see Greenleaf, R.K. and Spears, L.C. (2002). *Servant Leadership: A Journey into the Nature of Legitimate Power and Greatness*. 25th Anniversary Edition. Mahwah (NJ): Paulist Press; and Eva, N., Robin, M., Sendjaya, S., van Dierendonck, D. and Liden, R.C. (2019). "Servant Leadership: A Systematic Review and Call for Future Research." The Leadership Quarterly. 30(1).

CPSIA information can be obtained
at www.ICGtesting.com
Printed in the USA
BVHW020941181220
595878BV00014B/1060